■SCHOLASTIC

Extra Practice Math Centers

Multiplication, Division & More

BY **Mary Peterson**

D1451531

New York • Toronto • London • Auckland • Sydney
Mexico City • New Delhi • Hong Kong • Buenos Aires

Editor: Sarah Glasscock
Cover design by Lillian Kohli
Cover illustration by Kelly Kennedy
Interior design by Holly Grundon
Interior illustrations by Stephen Lewis

ISBN-13 978-0-439-69492-6
ISBN-10 0-439-69492-2

2 3 4 5 6 7 8 9 10   40   12 11 10 09 08

Contents

Introduction

Welcome to *Extra Practice Math Centers: Multiplication, Division, & More*. In my classroom, I find that many students need extra practice with math skills, even though we have to keep moving through the math curriculum. I created this collection of fun and interactive story problem cards, puzzles, and games to engage my students and give them the extra practice they need to master important math skills. These games have been tried and tested in my classroom. Children love them, beg for them, and will play them over and over. Teachers also love them because they can see the educational benefits.

How to Use These Extra Practice Math Centers

Math Center

After a game is introduced to a group, place it in a tub at the math center. Choice is highly motivating to students. The math center can be a choice during center time, or students can choose games or puzzles from the math center when they are finished with class assignments. This is a great way to keep them busy and independent. Students love the math center so much that it can be used as a reward. For example, everyone who brings back his or her math homework may have 15 minutes of extra math center time.

Rotating Math Stations

Students absolutely enjoy math stations. Divide the class into groups, and give each group a game. You can choose games that focus on the same math skill or a variety of skills. Every 10 to 15 minutes, rotate the games to a different group or rotate the students to a different station. If it is the first time you are introducing the games, invite parents or older students to the classroom to work at each station to give students extra support. This really helps things run smoothly. Then the games can be added to the math center for choice time.

Small-Group Instruction

You can use these games to reteach a skill or to give extra help to a small group of students. The students will become so engaged playing the game with you that they won't realize they are getting remedial help. Since the games are very self-explanatory, they are also useful for tutors or parent helpers working with individuals or small groups. The tutors will enjoy playing the games as much as the students.

Ten Key Educational Benefits

- Much more fun than "drill and kill"
- Significantly increases math achievement
- Instant engagement for students who say, "I'm finished, now what can I do?"
- Keeps students working independently while the teacher works with small groups
- Allows for student choice
- Gives students repeated math practice while they think they are just playing
- Supported by research on how children learn
- Gives students opportunities to work cooperatively
- Great rainy day math fun
- Inexpensive and easy to implement

The Games: How to Make and Store Them

For sturdy games that will last a long time, copy the pages onto card stock and then laminate them. If you copy all the pages for one game or puzzle on the same color of card stock, it will be easier to keep track of the pieces. Plastic storage bags work well for game storage because they hold all the small pieces. Attach the directions on the outside of the plastic storage bag with clear contact paper. Store all the games for the same math skill in a shoe box or tub so they can be located easily when you are ready to use them.

Story Problem Cards and Mats

These give students hands-on practice in solving story problems because they help students visualize how to solve a problem. Students can work in small groups or independently using the manipulatives to solve math problems. Store each story problem card and mat in a separate one-gallon-size plastic storage bag or a tub with the suggested manipulatives. I also suggest that you laminate them.

Board Games

The board games are very simple to play and a favorite of students. Players solve a math problem and then move around the board to be the first one to the end of the path. Most of the games have an answer key for self-checking. The board games are on two pages. They can be laminated separately and then taped together. When the game boards are folded in half, they will fit in a one-gallon-size plastic storage bag. Tape the directions for the game on the outside of the plastic storage bag. The game cards have a picture or words on the face to identify them. Keep everything needed to play the game in the same plastic storage bag. Good place markers for the games include different shapes and colors of erasers, plastic toys, pencil toppers, chess pieces, and leftover game pieces from old board games. Some games have spinners. A fast and easy way to make a spinner is to fasten a paper clip to the center of the spinner with a brass fastener. You can also purchase metal spinners at teacher supply stores.

Card Games

The card games are simple yet fun to play and are modeled after many of the old favorites. Using a different color of card stock for each game will help you keep the games separate, and identifying words or pictures appear on the face of each card. Cut apart the cards and keep them and all other materials needed for the game in a one-quart-size plastic storage bag. Attach the game directions to the front of the bag.

Puzzles

The puzzles can be pieced together independently or with a partner. Students enjoy being able to self-check their answers by seeing if the puzzle is put together correctly. When copying the puzzles, make sure to copy the picture on the back of the answer cards. Copy each puzzle on a different color of card stock, as these pieces can get mixed up easily. Cut apart the cards with the picture on the back. Students read the math problem on the game board and cover it with the correct answer card. Then they flip over the answer cards. If the answers are correct, the picture puzzle has been put together correctly. Keep each game board and accompanying puzzle pieces in a separate plastic storage bag. Attach the directions and a small picture of the completed puzzle on the outside.

Multiplication Centers

Story Problem Cards and Mats

....

Puzzles

....

Board Games

....

Card Games

....

Story Problem Cards and Mats

Directions:

1. Laminate the five story problem cards on pages 8, 12, 14, 16, and 19, and the corresponding mats.

2. Use an overhead marker to write multiplication problems on the cards. (Change the numbers by wiping off the marker.)

3. Have students place manipulatives on the corresponding story mat(s) to create the equal groups described on each story problem card. After solving the problem with manipulatives, students illustrate and write the answer in their math journals.

School Bus, pp. 8–11: Students put an equal number of children on each bus. Then they figure out how many children there are.

Manipulatives: dried beans with faces drawn on them or smiley-face erasers

Cookies, pp. 12–13: Students create an array of cookies in rows and columns on the cookie sheet grid and then find out how many cookies there are.

Manipulatives: cereal pieces or miniature cookies (Students can eat them when the problem is solved!)

Piggy Bank, pp. 14–15: Write the number of pennies, nickels, and/or dimes to go in the piggy bank. (Example: In your piggy bank, you have 7 nickels.) Students multiply or count by 1s, 5s, or 10s to find how much money they have.

Manipulatives: plastic or real coins

Buttons, pp. 16–18: Students put an equal number of buttons on each shirt and then count all the buttons.

Manipulatives: buttons or small, round beans

Bear Houses, pp. 19–22: Students place an equal number of bears in each house and then find out how many bears there are all together.

Manipulatives: plastic bears or bear crackers

There are _____ school buses

with _____ children on each bus.

How many children are there

on all the buses?

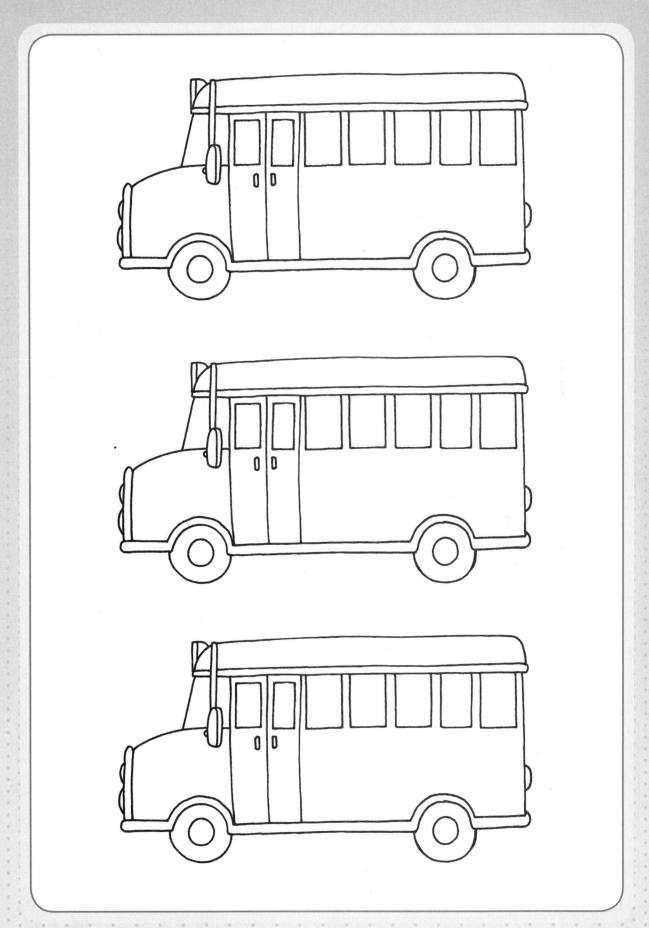

Mom is baking cookies. She asks you

to place _____

_____ rows and

columns of cookies on the cookie sheet.

How many cookies will be

on the cookie sheet?

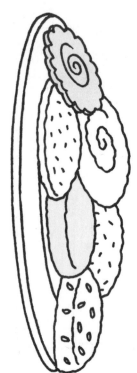

 Extra Practice Math Centers: Multiplication, Division, & More © 2007 by Mary Peterson, Scholastic Teaching Resources

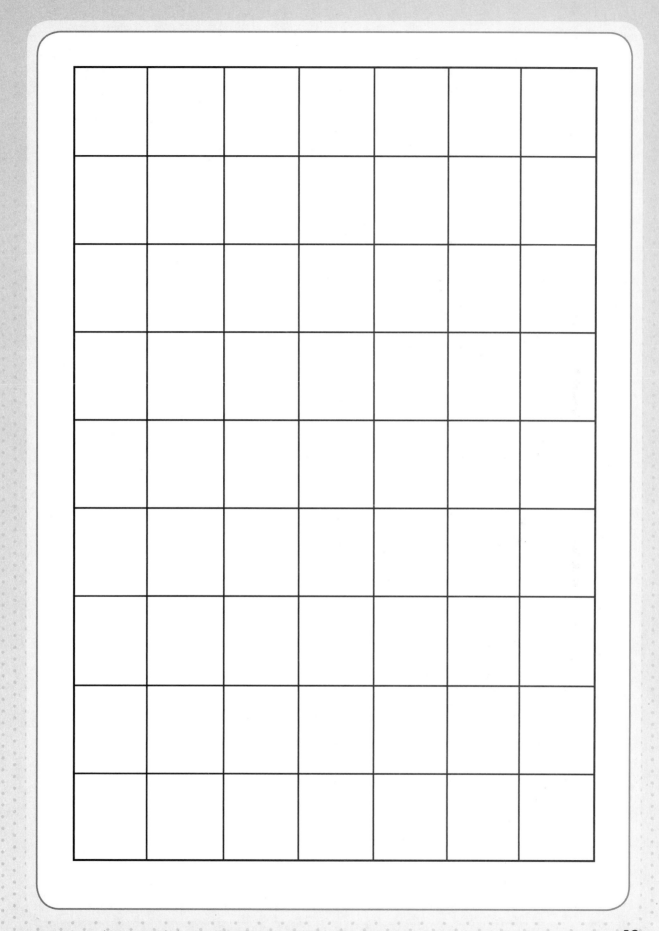

In your piggy bank, you
have _____ .

How much money
do you have?

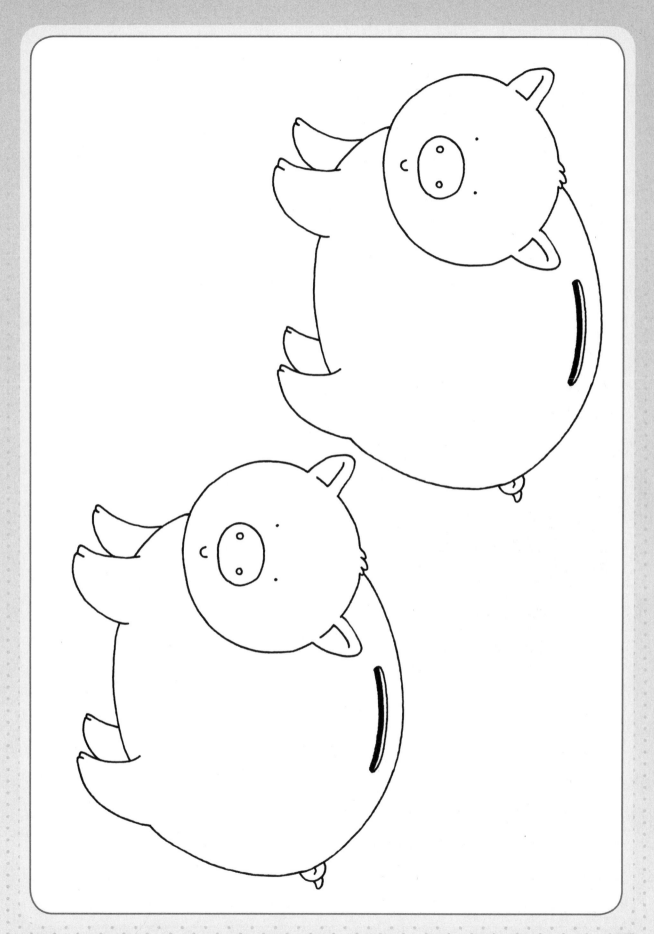

Aunt Jane is making —————— shirts.

She asks you to put —————— buttons

on each shirt.

How many buttons

do you need?

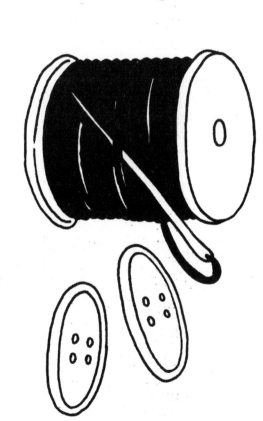

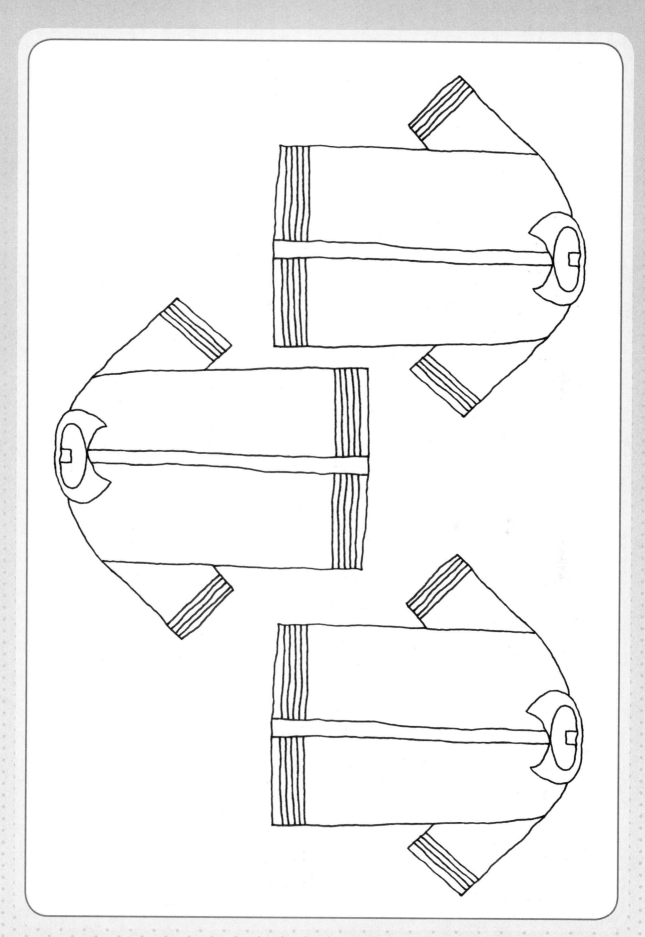

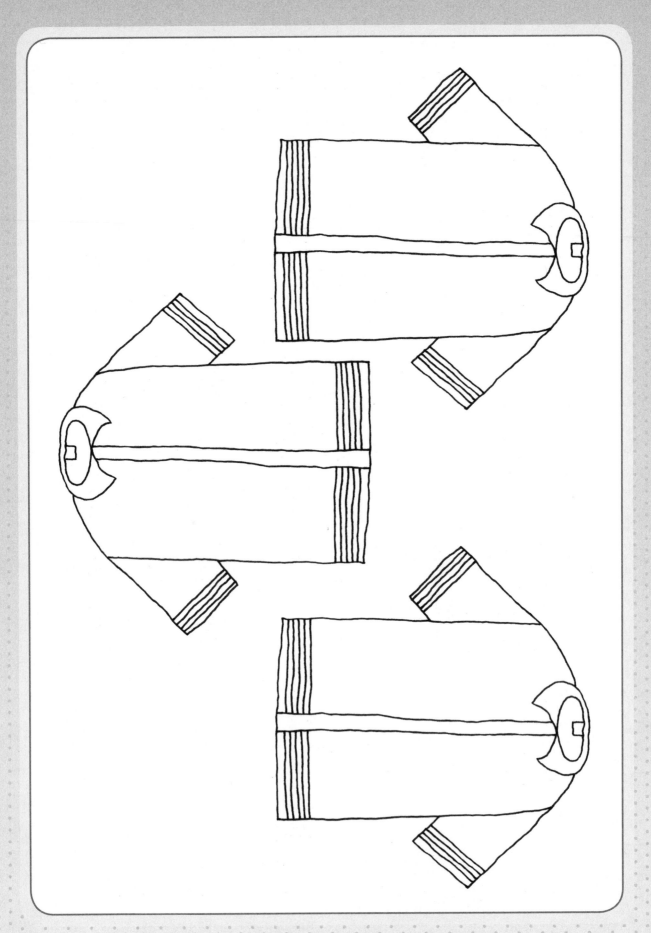

There are _____ _____ houses.

_____ bears live in each house.

How many bears

are there all

together?

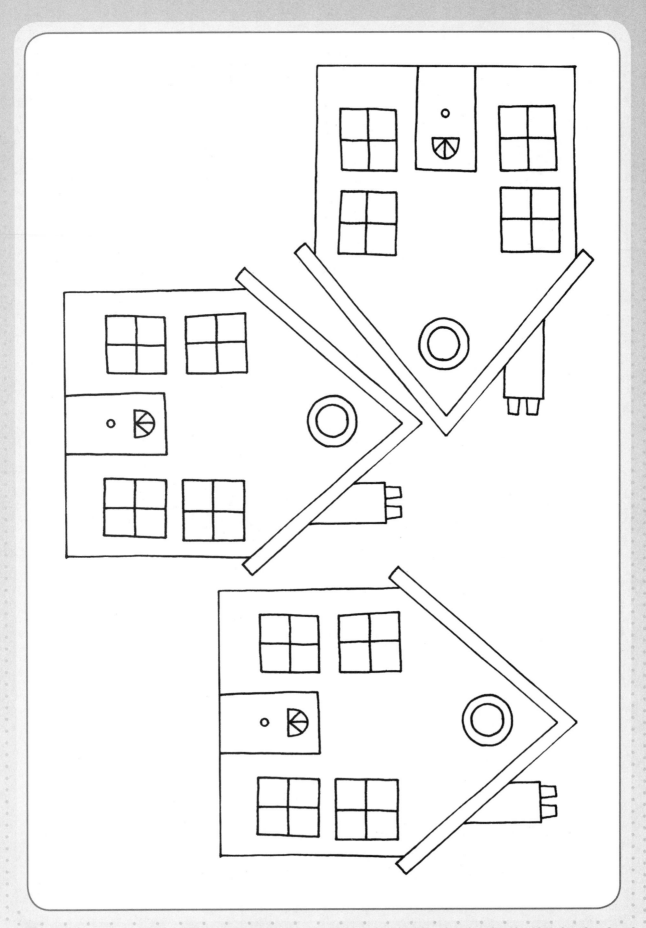

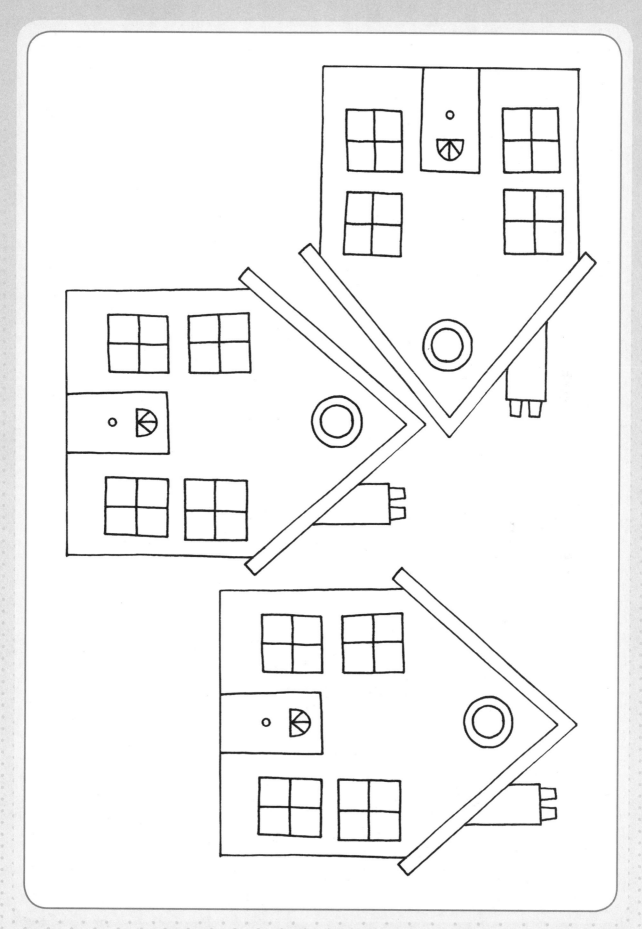

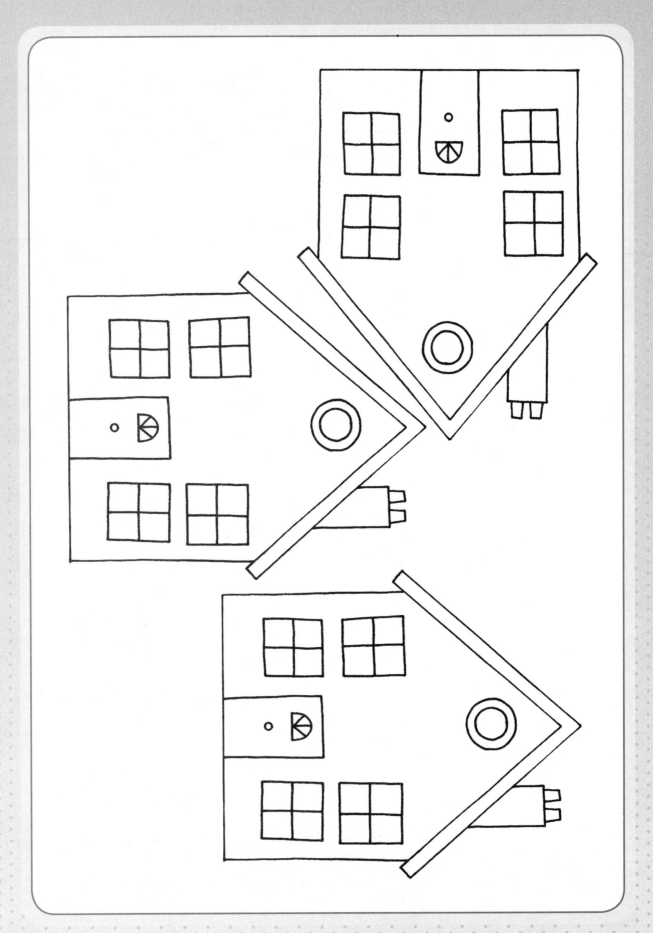

Multiplication Puzzles

Directions:

1. For each puzzle, make a two-sided copy with the picture puzzle on one side and the answer cards on the other side. Cut apart the answer cards. (Note: Copy each puzzle onto a different color of card stock.)

2. The page that shows the corresponding multiplication expressions is the game board (pp. 24, 27, 30).

3. Students read a multiplication expression on the game board. Then they cover it with the correct answer card.

4. When answer cards cover the entire game board, students turn over the cards. If the picture puzzle is put together correctly, all the products are correct. If the puzzle is not put together correctly, have students check the multiplication grid below to find the correct products.

×	1	2	3	4	5	6	7	8	9
1	1	2	3	4	5	6	7	8	9
2	2	4	6	8	10	12	14	16	18
3	3	6	9	12	15	18	21	24	27
4	4	8	12	16	20	24	28	32	36
5	5	10	15	20	25	30	35	40	45
6	6	12	18	24	30	36	42	48	54
7	7	14	21	28	35	42	49	56	63
8	8	16	24	32	40	48	56	64	72
9	9	18	27	36	45	54	63	72	81

Multiplication Puzzle 1 Game Board

Multiplication Puzzle 1 **9 x 9**	Multiplication Puzzle 1 **7 x 3**	Multiplication Puzzle 1 **2 x 5**
Multiplication Puzzle 1 **7 x 8**	Multiplication Puzzle 1 **5 x 7**	Multiplication Puzzle 1 **7 x 7**
Multiplication Puzzle 1 **3 x 9**	Multiplication Puzzle 1 **8 x 8**	Multiplication Puzzle 1 **8 x 9**
Multiplication Puzzle 1 **5 x 5**	Multiplication Puzzle 1 **9 x 5**	Multiplication Puzzle 1 **6 x 4**
Multiplication Puzzle 1 **8 x 4**	Multiplication Puzzle 1 **9 x 6**	Multiplication Puzzle 1 **6 x 7**

 Extra Practice Math Centers: Multiplication, Division, & More © 2007 by Mary Peterson, Scholastic Teaching Resources

Multiplication Puzzle 1 Answer Cards

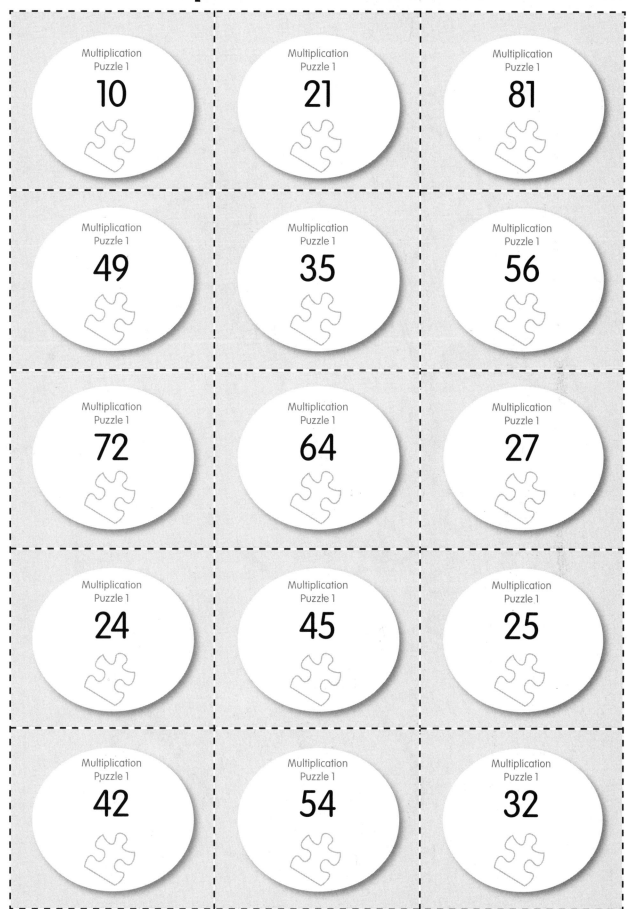

Multiplication Puzzle 1
10

Multiplication Puzzle 1
21

Multiplication Puzzle 1
81

Multiplication Puzzle 1
49

Multiplication Puzzle 1
35

Multiplication Puzzle 1
56

Multiplication Puzzle 1
72

Multiplication Puzzle 1
64

Multiplication Puzzle 1
27

Multiplication Puzzle 1
24

Multiplication Puzzle 1
45

Multiplication Puzzle 1
25

Multiplication Puzzle 1
42

Multiplication Puzzle 1
54

Multiplication Puzzle 1
32

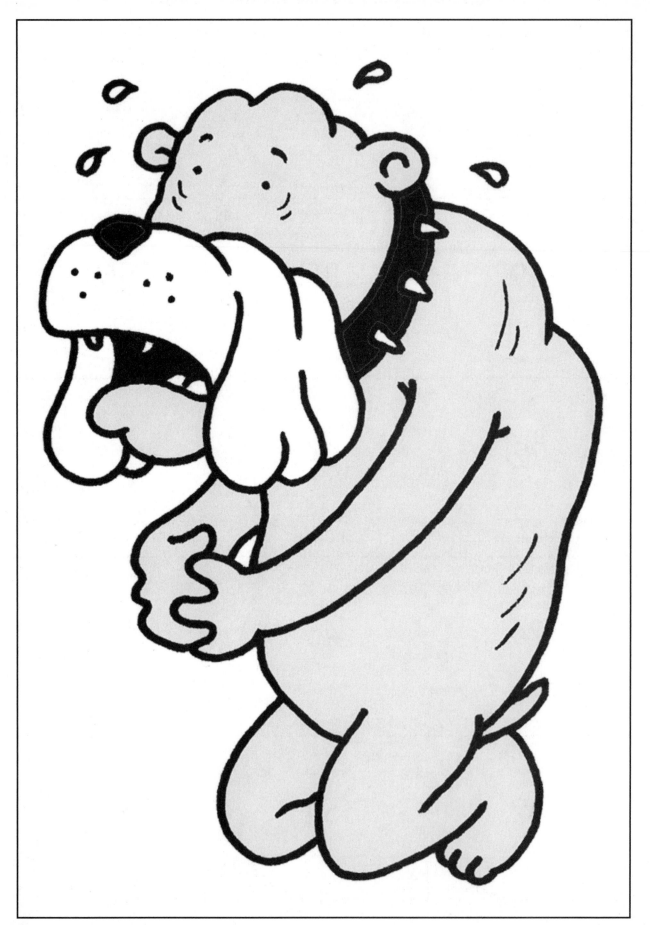

Extra Practice Math Centers: Multiplication, Division, & More © 2007 by Mary Peterson, Scholastic Teaching Resources

Multiplication Puzzle 2 Game Board

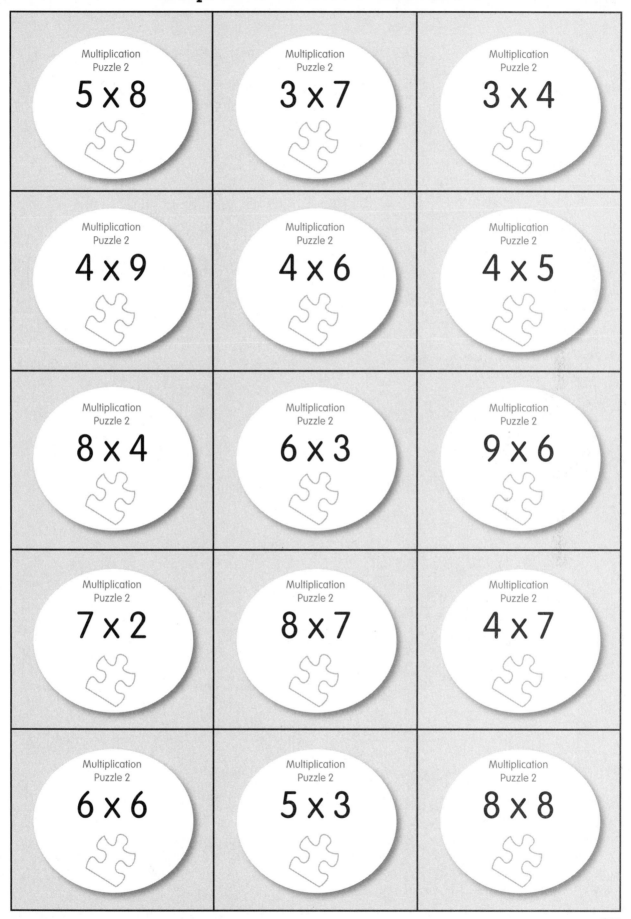

Multiplication Puzzle 2 **5 x 8**	Multiplication Puzzle 2 **3 x 7**	Multiplication Puzzle 2 **3 x 4**
Multiplication Puzzle 2 **4 x 9**	Multiplication Puzzle 2 **4 x 6**	Multiplication Puzzle 2 **4 x 5**
Multiplication Puzzle 2 **8 x 4**	Multiplication Puzzle 2 **6 x 3**	Multiplication Puzzle 2 **9 x 6**
Multiplication Puzzle 2 **7 x 2**	Multiplication Puzzle 2 **8 x 7**	Multiplication Puzzle 2 **4 x 7**
Multiplication Puzzle 2 **6 x 6**	Multiplication Puzzle 2 **5 x 3**	Multiplication Puzzle 2 **8 x 8**

Multiplication Puzzle 2 Answer Cards

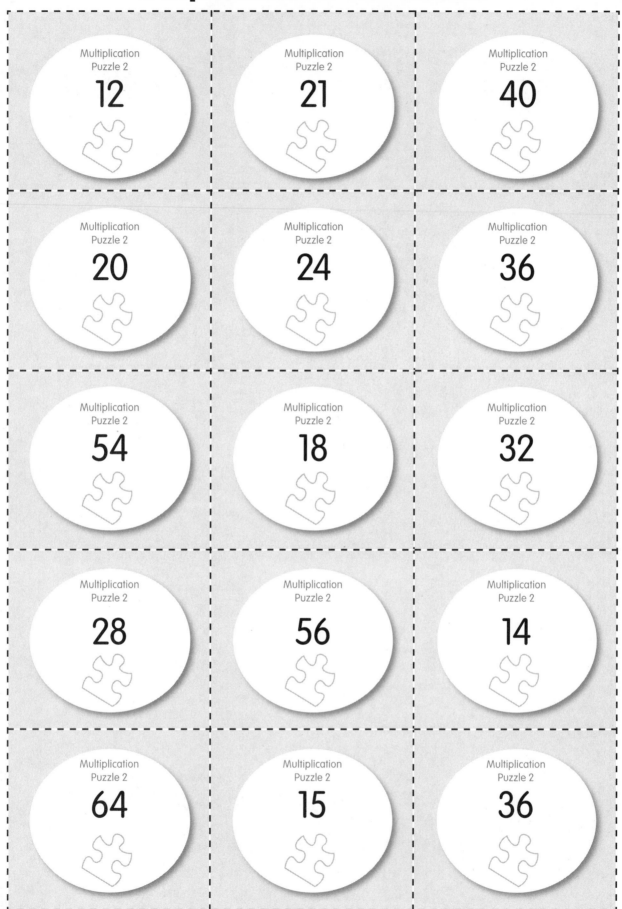

Multiplication Puzzle 2
12

Multiplication Puzzle 2
21

Multiplication Puzzle 2
40

Multiplication Puzzle 2
20

Multiplication Puzzle 2
24

Multiplication Puzzle 2
36

Multiplication Puzzle 2
54

Multiplication Puzzle 2
18

Multiplication Puzzle 2
32

Multiplication Puzzle 2
28

Multiplication Puzzle 2
56

Multiplication Puzzle 2
14

Multiplication Puzzle 2
64

Multiplication Puzzle 2
15

Multiplication Puzzle 2
36

Extra Practice Math Centers: Multiplication, Division, & More © 2007 by Mary Peterson, Scholastic Teaching Resources

Multiplication Puzzle 3 Game Board

Multiplication
Puzzle 3

5 x 8

Multiplication
Puzzle 3

6 x 9

Multiplication
Puzzle 3

6 x 7

Multiplication
Puzzle 3

5 x 7

Multiplication
Puzzle 3

3 x 3

Multiplication
Puzzle 3

4 x 4

Multiplication
Puzzle 3

2 x 7

Multiplication
Puzzle 3

6 x 6

Multiplication
Puzzle 3

6 x 2

Multiplication
Puzzle 3

3 x 5

Multiplication
Puzzle 3

5 x 5

Multiplication
Puzzle 3

6 x 8

Multiplication
Puzzle 3

4 x 5

Multiplication
Puzzle 3

5 x 9

Multiplication
Puzzle 3

3 x 9

Multiplication Puzzle 3 Answer Cards

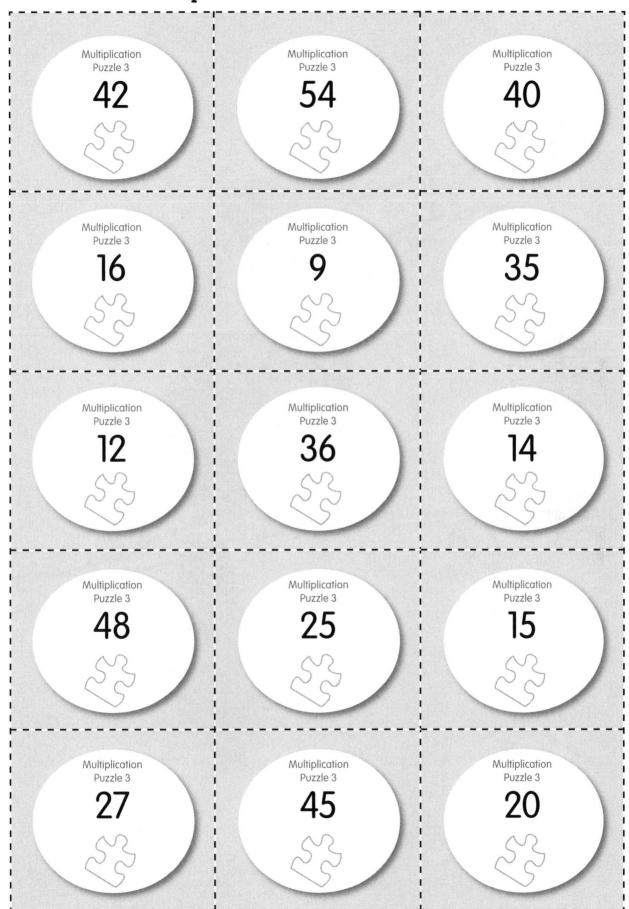

Multiplication
Puzzle 3

42

Multiplication
Puzzle 3

54

Multiplication
Puzzle 3

40

Multiplication
Puzzle 3

16

Multiplication
Puzzle 3

9

Multiplication
Puzzle 3

35

Multiplication
Puzzle 3

12

Multiplication
Puzzle 3

36

Multiplication
Puzzle 3

14

Multiplication
Puzzle 3

48

Multiplication
Puzzle 3

25

Multiplication
Puzzle 3

15

Multiplication
Puzzle 3

27

Multiplication
Puzzle 3

45

Multiplication
Puzzle 3

20

Times Track

Directions:

1. Players place their markers on Start.

2. They take turns spinning a number and moving that number of spaces around the track.

3. Then the player draws a card and multiplies the number on the card by the number on the space where he or she landed. Another player uses the multiplication grid to check the answer. If the answer is incorrect, the player goes back to the square he or she was on.

4. The first person to go around the track two times is the winner.

X	1	2	3	4	5	6	7	8	9
1	1	2	3	4	5	6	7	8	9
2	2	4	6	8	10	12	14	16	18
3	3	6	9	12	15	18	21	24	27
4	4	8	12	16	20	24	28	32	36
5	5	10	15	20	25	30	35	40	45
6	6	12	18	24	30	36	42	48	54
7	7	14	21	28	35	42	49	56	63
8	8	16	24	32	40	48	56	64	72
9	9	18	27	36	45	54	63	72	81

Times Track

Start

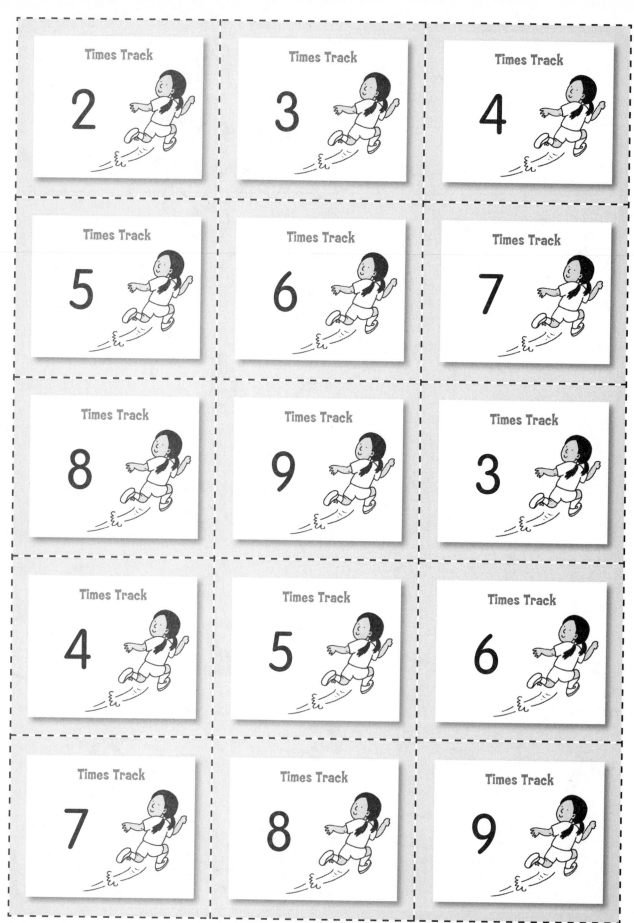

MonKey Multiplication

Directions:

1. Players place their markers on Start.

2. They take turns drawing a card and solving the multiplication problem on it.

3. Another player uses the multiplication grid to check the answer. If the product is correct, the player may move the number of spaces on the card.

4. The first person to get his or her marker to the banana is the winner.

×	1	2	3	4	5	6	7	8	9
1	1	2	3	4	5	6	7	8	9
2	2	4	6	8	10	12	14	16	18
3	3	6	9	12	15	18	21	24	27
4	4	8	12	16	20	24	28	32	36
5	5	10	15	20	25	30	35	40	45
6	6	12	18	24	30	36	42	48	54
7	7	14	21	28	35	42	49	56	63
8	8	16	24	32	40	48	56	64	72
9	9	18	27	36	45	54	63	72	81

Extra Practice Math Centers: Multiplication, Division, & More © 2007 by Mary Peterson, Scholastic Teaching Resources

MonKey

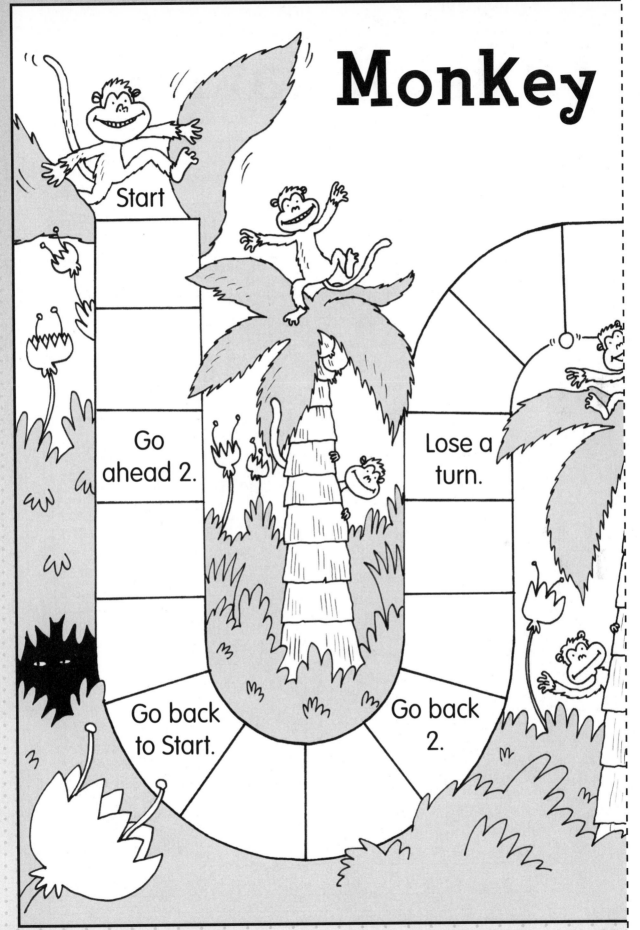

Start

Go ahead 2.

Lose a turn.

Go back to Start.

Go back 2.

Multiplication

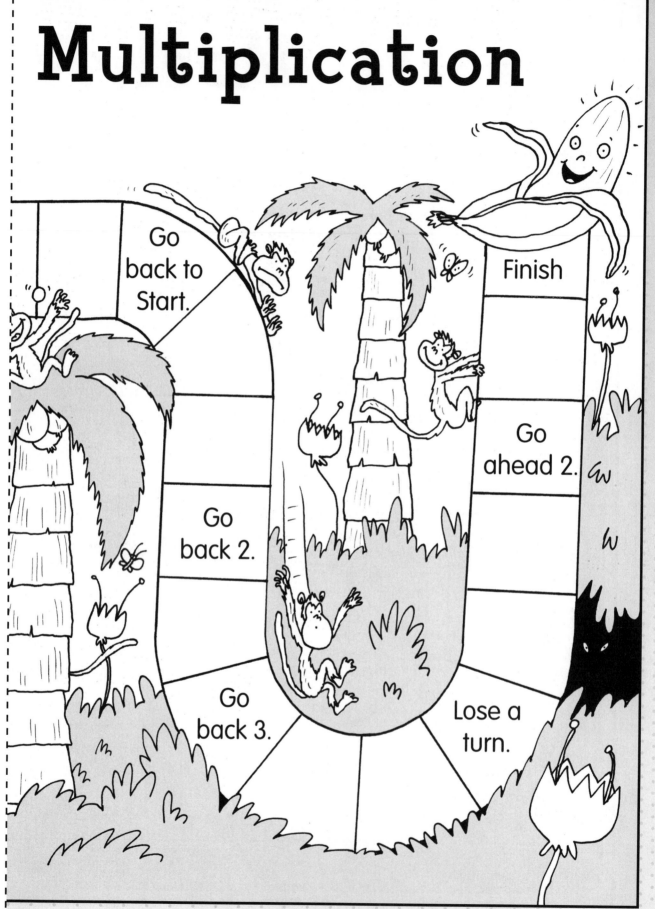

Go back to Start.

Finish

Go back 2.

Go ahead 2.

Go back 3.

Lose a turn.

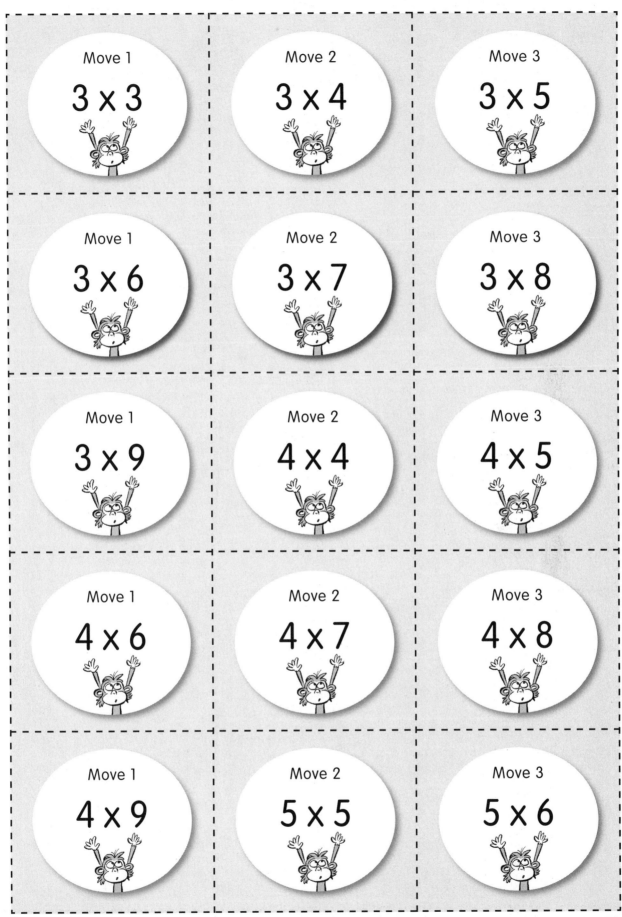

Move 1
3 x 3

Move 2
3 x 4

Move 3
3 x 5

Move 1
3 x 6

Move 2
3 x 7

Move 3
3 x 8

Move 1
3 x 9

Move 2
4 x 4

Move 3
4 x 5

Move 1
4 x 6

Move 2
4 x 7

Move 3
4 x 8

Move 1
4 x 9

Move 2
5 x 5

Move 3
5 x 6

Move 1

5 x 7

Move 2

5 x 8

Move 3

5 x 9

Move 1

6 x 6

Move 2

6 x 7

Move 3

6 x 8

Move 1

6 x 9

Move 2

7 x 7

Move 3

7 x 8

Move 1

7 x 9

Move 2

8 x 8

Move 3

8 x 9

Move 1

9 x 9

Move 2

2 x 8

Move 3

2 x 7

Multiplication Concentration

Directions:

1. Duplicate the pages of multiplication expressions on one color of card stock and corresponding products on a different color.

2. Shuffle one or more sets of game cards, and then place them facedown in rows.

3. Players take turns turning over two cards, one of each color. If the cards form a correct multiplication equation, the player keeps the cards and takes another turn.

4. If the cards do not match, the player turns them over. The next player takes a turn.

5. When all the matches have been made, the player with the most cards is the winner.

✕	1	2	3	4	5	6	7	8	9
1	1	2	3	4	5	6	7	8	9
2	2	4	6	8	10	12	14	16	18
3	3	6	9	12	15	18	21	24	27
4	4	8	12	16	20	24	28	32	36
5	5	10	15	20	25	30	35	40	45
6	6	12	18	24	30	36	42	48	54
7	7	14	21	28	35	42	49	56	63
8	8	16	24	32	40	48	56	64	72
9	9	18	27	36	45	54	63	72	81

Multiplication Concentration

3×5

Multiplication Concentration

3×6

Multiplication Concentration

3×7

Multiplication Concentration

3×8

Multiplication Concentration

3×9

Multiplication Concentration

4×4

Multiplication Concentration

4×5

Multiplication Concentration

4×6

Multiplication Concentration

4×7

Multiplication Concentration

4×8

Extra Practice Math Centers: Multiplication, Division, & More © 2007 by Mary Peterson, Scholastic Teaching Resources

Multiplication Concentration	Multiplication Concentration
15	18
Multiplication Concentration	Multiplication Concentration
21	24
Multiplication Concentration	Multiplication Concentration
27	16
Multiplication Concentration	Multiplication Concentration
20	24
Multiplication Concentration	Multiplication Concentration
28	32

Multiplication Concentration	Multiplication Concentration
4 x 9	5 x 5
Multiplication Concentration	Multiplication Concentration
5 x 6	5 x 7
Multiplication Concentration	Multiplication Concentration
5 x 8	5 x 9
Multiplication Concentration	Multiplication Concentration
6 x 6	6 x 7
Multiplication Concentration	Multiplication Concentration
6 x 8	6 x 9

 Extra Practice Math Centers: Multiplication, Division, & More © 2007 by Mary Peterson, Scholastic Teaching Resources

Multiplication Concentration	Multiplication Concentration
36	25
Multiplication Concentration	Multiplication Concentration
30	35
Multiplication Concentration	Multiplication Concentration
40	45
Multiplication Concentration	Multiplication Concentration
36	42
Multiplication Concentration	Multiplication Concentration
48	54

Multiplication Concentration	Multiplication Concentration
2 x 2	2 x 3
Multiplication Concentration	Multiplication Concentration
2 x 4	2 x 5
Multiplication Concentration	Multiplication Concentration
2 x 6	2 x 7
Multiplication Concentration	Multiplication Concentration
2 x 8	2 x 9
Multiplication Concentration	**Multiplication Concentration**
3 x 3	3 x 4

Multiplication Concentration	Multiplication Concentration
4	6
Multiplication Concentration	Multiplication Concentration
8	10
Multiplication Concentration	Multiplication Concentration
12	14
Multiplication Concentration	Multiplication Concentration
16	18
Multiplication Concentration	Multiplication Concentration
9	12

Multiplication Concentration	Multiplication Concentration
7×7	7×8
Multiplication Concentration	Multiplication Concentration
7×9	8×8
Multiplication Concentration	Multiplication Concentration
8×9	9×9
Multiplication Concentration	Multiplication Concentration
1×9	1×8
Multiplication Concentration	Multiplication Concentration
1×7	1×6

Multiplication Concentration	Multiplication Concentration
49	56
Multiplication Concentration	Multiplication Concentration
63	64
Multiplication Concentration	Multiplication Concentration
72	81
Multiplication Concentration	Multiplication Concentration
9	8
Multiplication Concentration	Multiplication Concentration
7	6

Fact Family Rummy

Directions:

1. Shuffle the cards. Then deal five cards to each player. Place the remaining cards facedown in a pile.

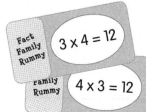

2. Players take turns drawing a card. When a player gets a complete fact family of four cards, he or she sets the cards faceup on the table.

3. At the end of each turn, the player discards one card and places it faceup in the discard pile. The next player may draw either a card from the discard pile or a facedown card from the other pile.

4. The first player to get rid of all the cards in his or her hand is the winner.

Fact Families			
3 x 4 = 12	4 x 3 = 12	12 ÷ 4 = 3	12 ÷ 3 = 4
5 x 4 = 20	4 x 5 = 20	20 ÷ 4 = 5	20 ÷ 5 = 4
6 x 7 = 42	7 x 6 = 42	42 ÷ 7 = 6	42 ÷ 6 = 7
8 x 7 = 56	7 x 8 = 56	56 ÷ 7 = 8	56 ÷ 8 = 7
9 x 6 = 54	6 x 9 = 54	54 ÷ 9 = 6	54 ÷ 6 = 9
4 x 9 = 36	9 x 4 = 36	36 ÷ 4 = 9	36 ÷ 9 = 4
5 x 7 = 35	7 x 5 = 35	35 ÷ 7 = 5	35 ÷ 5 = 7
6 x 3 = 18	3 x 6 = 18	18 ÷ 6 = 3	18 ÷ 3 = 6
8 x 6 = 48	6 x 8 = 48	48 ÷ 8 = 6	48 ÷ 6 = 8
9 x 7 = 63	7 x 9 = 63	63 ÷ 7 = 9	63 ÷ 9 = 7

Extra Practice Math Centers: Multiplication, Division, & More © 2007 by Mary Peterson, Scholastic Teaching Resources

Fact Family Rummy	$3 \times 4 = 12$	Fact Family Rummy	$4 \times 3 = 12$
Fact Family Rummy	$12 \div 4 = 3$	Fact Family Rummy	$12 \div 3 = 4$
Fact Family Rummy	$5 \times 4 = 20$	Fact Family Rummy	$4 \times 5 = 20$
Fact Family Rummy	$20 \div 5 = 4$	Fact Family Rummy	$20 \div 4 = 5$
Fact Family Rummy	$6 \times 7 = 42$	Fact Family Rummy	$7 \times 6 = 42$

Fact Family Rummy	$42 \div 6 = 7$	Fact Family Rummy	$42 \div 7 = 6$
Fact Family Rummy	$8 \times 7 = 56$	Fact Family Rummy	$7 \times 8 = 56$
Fact Family Rummy	$56 \div 8 = 7$	Fact Family Rummy	$56 \div 7 = 8$
Fact Family Rummy	$9 \times 6 = 54$	Fact Family Rummy	$6 \times 9 = 54$
Fact Family Rummy	$54 \div 9 = 6$	Fact Family Rummy	$54 \div 6 = 9$

 Extra Practice Math Centers: Multiplication, Division, & More © 2007 by Mary Peterson, Scholastic Teaching Resources

Fact Family Rummy

$4 \times 9 = 36$

Fact Family Rummy

$9 \times 4 = 36$

Fact Family Rummy

$36 \div 9 = 4$

Fact Family Rummy

$36 \div 4 = 9$

Fact Family Rummy

$5 \times 7 = 35$

Fact Family Rummy

$7 \times 5 = 35$

Fact Family Rummy

$35 \div 7 = 5$

Fact Family Rummy

$35 \div 5 = 7$

Fact Family Rummy

$6 \times 3 = 18$

Fact Family Rummy

$3 \times 6 = 18$

Fact Family Rummy	$18 \div 6 = 3$	Fact Family Rummy	$18 \div 3 = 6$
Fact Family Rummy	$6 \times 8 = 48$	Fact Family Rummy	$8 \times 6 = 48$
Fact Family Rummy	$48 \div 6 = 8$	Fact Family Rummy	$48 \div 8 = 6$
Fact Family Rummy	$9 \times 7 = 63$	Fact Family Rummy	$7 \times 9 = 63$
Fact Family Rummy	$63 \div 7 = 9$	Fact Family Rummy	$63 \div 9 = 7$

Extra Practice Math Centers: Multiplication, Division, & More © 2007 by Mary Peterson, Scholastic Teaching Resources

Division Centers

Story Problem Cards and Mats

Puzzles

Board Games

Card Games

Triominoes

Story Problem Cards and Mats

Directions:

1. Laminate the four story problem cards on pages 59, 62, 64, and 66.

2. Use an overhead marker to write division problems on the cards. (Change the numbers by wiping off the marker.)

3. Have students place manipulatives on the corresponding story mat(s) to create the equal groups described on each story problem card. After solving the problem with manipulatives, students illustrate and write the answer in their math journals.

Fish, pp. 59–61: Students divide the fish equally among the fish bowls to figure out how many fish go in each bowl and how many fish will be left over.

Manipulatives: fish-shaped erasers or fish crackers

Cars, pp. 62–63: Students place the cars into equal rows on the parking lot grid to decide how many cars will be in each row and how many cars will be left over.

Manipulatives: erasers shaped like small cars

Children, pp. 64–65: Students line up children in equal rows on the grid to find out how many children will be in each row and if any children will be left over.

Manipulatives: small smiley-face erasers

Dog Bones, pp. 66–68: Students divide bones equally among the dogs to figure out how many bones each dog gets and if there are any bones remaining.

Manipulatives: dried beans or small dog biscuits

You have _____ pet fish.

Place an equal number of fish into

_____ fish bowls. How many fish

are in each bowl?

Are there any

remaining fish?

There are _____ cars to be parked.

Put them in _____ equal rows.

How many cars are in each row? Are there any remaining cars?

School Parking Lot

_____ children will march in the parade. They will march in _____ equal rows. How many children are in each row? Are there any children left over?

Extra Practice Math Centers: Multiplication, Division, & More © 2007 by Mary Peterson, Scholastic Teaching Resources

Parade

You have _____ bones to share

with _____ dogs. How many bones

will each dog get?

Will any bones be

left over?

Extra Practice Math Centers: Multiplication, Division, & More © 2007 by Mary Peterson, Scholastic Teaching Resources

 Extra Practice Math Centers: Multiplication, Division, & More © 2007 by Mary Peterson, Scholastic Teaching Resources

Dinosaur Division

Directions:

1. Players place their markers on Start.

2. Players take turns drawing a dinosaur card. They must solve the division problem on the card and move their marker to the nearest square with that quotient. Answers can be checked on the multiplication/division grid.

3. The first player to reach the palm tree is the winner.

X	1	2	3	4	5	6	7	8	9
1	1	2	3	4	5	6	7	8	9
2	2	4	6	8	10	12	14	16	18
3	3	6	9	12	15	18	21	24	27
4	4	8	12	16	20	24	28	32	36
5	5	10	15	20	25	30	35	40	45
6	6	12	18	24	30	36	42	48	54
7	7	14	21	28	35	42	49	56	63
8	8	16	24	32	40	48	56	64	72
9	9	18	27	36	45	54	63	72	81

Dinosaur

Start

| 1 | 2 | 3 | 4 | 5 | 6 | 7 | 8 | 9 |

| 1 | 9 | 8 | 7 | 6 | 5 | 4 | 3 | 2 |

| 2 |

| 3 | 4 | 5 | 6 | 7 | 8 | 9 | 1 | 2 |

| 3 | 2 | 1 | 9 | 8 | 7 | 6 | 5 | 4 |

| 4 |

| 5 | 6 | 7 | 8 | 9 | 1 | 2 | 3 | 4 |

Finish

| 1 | 9 | 8 | 7 | 6 |

Division

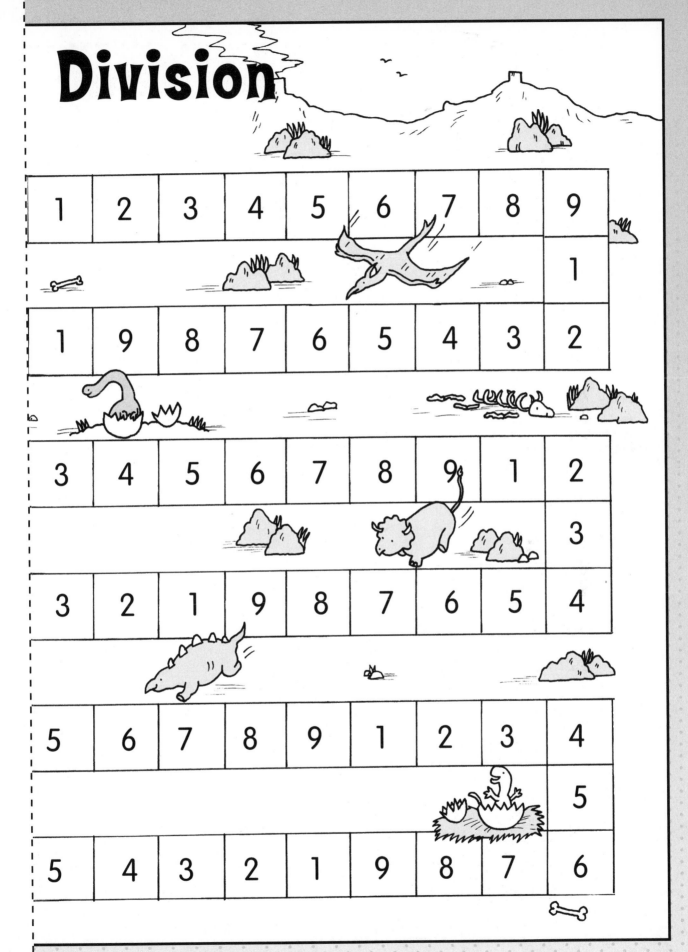

1	2	3	4	5	6	7	8	9

								1

1	9	8	7	6	5	4	3	2

3	4	5	6	7	8	9	1	2

								3

3	2	1	9	8	7	6	5	4

5	6	7	8	9	1	2	3	4

								5

5	4	3	2	1	9	8	7	6

Dinosaur Division

1 ÷ 1

Dinosaur Division

2 ÷ 2

Dinosaur Division

3 ÷ 3

Dinosaur Division

4 ÷ 4

Dinosaur Division

5 ÷ 5

Dinosaur Division

6 ÷ 6

Dinosaur Division

7 ÷ 7

Dinosaur Division

8 ÷ 8

Dinosaur Division

9 ÷ 9

Dinosaur Division

2 ÷ 1

Dinosaur Division

4 ÷ 2

Dinosaur Division

6 ÷ 3

Dinosaur Division

8 ÷ 4

Dinosaur Division

10 ÷ 5

Dinosaur Division

12 ÷ 6

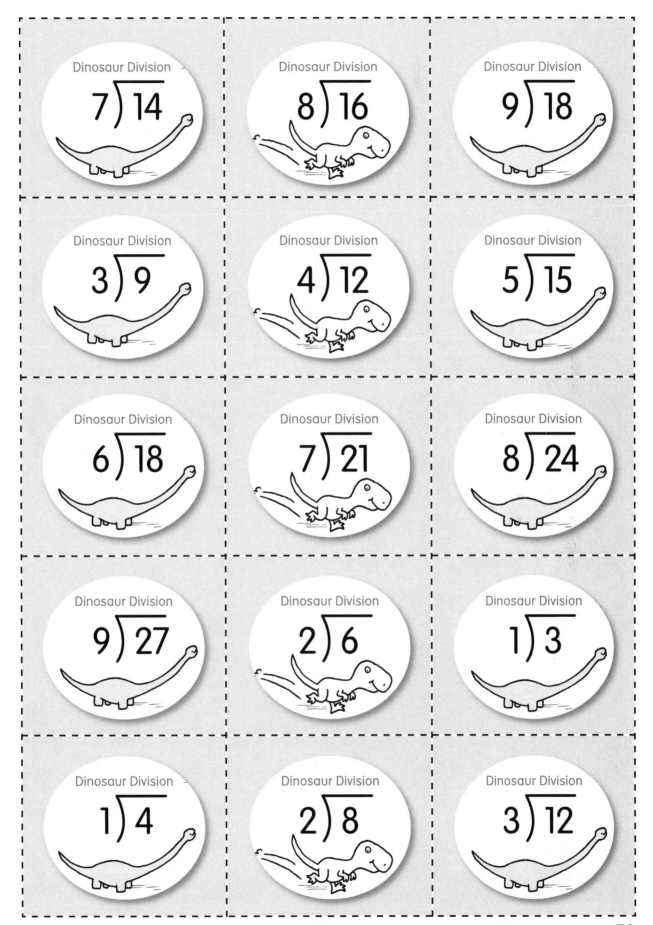

Dinosaur Division
$7 \overline{)14}$

Dinosaur Division
$8 \overline{)16}$

Dinosaur Division
$9 \overline{)18}$

Dinosaur Division
$3 \overline{)9}$

Dinosaur Division
$4 \overline{)12}$

Dinosaur Division
$5 \overline{)15}$

Dinosaur Division
$6 \overline{)18}$

Dinosaur Division
$7 \overline{)21}$

Dinosaur Division
$8 \overline{)24}$

Dinosaur Division
$9 \overline{)27}$

Dinosaur Division
$2 \overline{)6}$

Dinosaur Division
$1 \overline{)3}$

Dinosaur Division
$1 \overline{)4}$

Dinosaur Division
$2 \overline{)8}$

Dinosaur Division
$3 \overline{)12}$

Dinosaur Division	Dinosaur Division	Dinosaur Division
16 ÷ 4	20 ÷ 5	24 ÷ 6
Dinosaur Division	Dinosaur Division	Dinosaur Division
28 ÷ 7	32 ÷ 8	36 ÷ 9
Dinosaur Division	Dinosaur Division	Dinosaur Division
5 ÷ 1	10 ÷ 2	15 ÷ 3
Dinosaur Division	Dinosaur Division	Dinosaur Division
20 ÷ 4	25 ÷ 5	30 ÷ 6
Dinosaur Division	Dinosaur Division	Dinosaur Division
35 ÷ 7	40 ÷ 8	45 ÷ 9

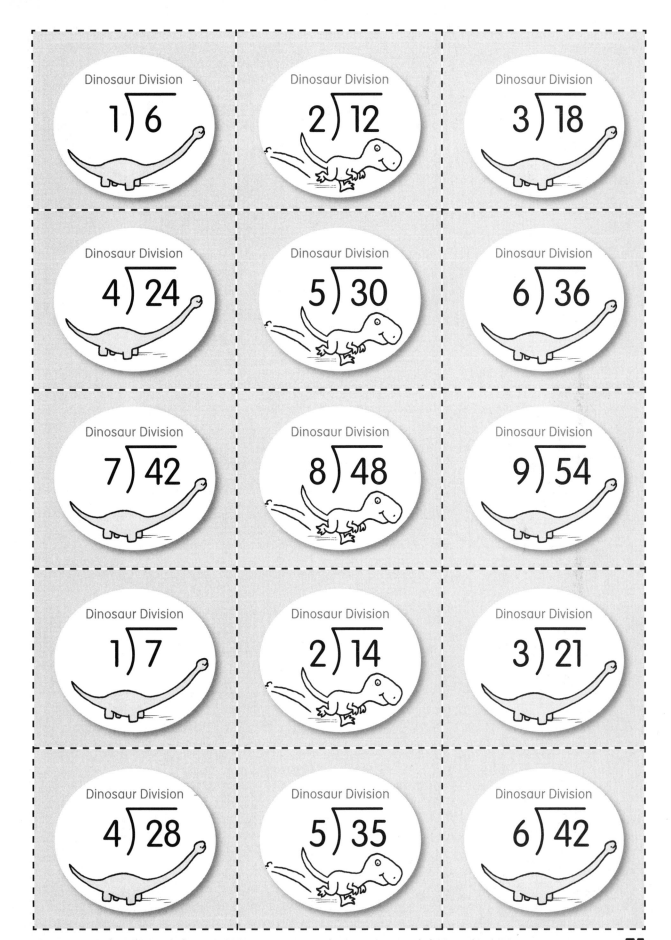

Dinosaur Division
$$1\overline{)6}$$

Dinosaur Division
$$2\overline{)12}$$

Dinosaur Division
$$3\overline{)18}$$

Dinosaur Division
$$4\overline{)24}$$

Dinosaur Division
$$5\overline{)30}$$

Dinosaur Division
$$6\overline{)36}$$

Dinosaur Division
$$7\overline{)42}$$

Dinosaur Division
$$8\overline{)48}$$

Dinosaur Division
$$9\overline{)54}$$

Dinosaur Division
$$1\overline{)7}$$

Dinosaur Division
$$2\overline{)14}$$

Dinosaur Division
$$3\overline{)21}$$

Dinosaur Division
$$4\overline{)28}$$

Dinosaur Division
$$5\overline{)35}$$

Dinosaur Division
$$6\overline{)42}$$

Dinosaur Division

49 ÷ 7

Dinosaur Division

56 ÷ 8

Dinosaur Division

63 ÷ 9

Dinosaur Division

16 ÷ 2

Dinosaur Division

24 ÷ 3

Dinosaur Division

32 ÷ 4

Dinosaur Division

48 ÷ 6

Dinosaur Division

64 ÷ 8

Dinosaur Division

72 ÷ 9

Dinosaur Division

27 ÷ 3

Dinosaur Division

36 ÷ 4

Dinosaur Division

45 ÷ 5

Dinosaur Division

54 ÷ 6

Dinosaur Division

72 ÷ 8

Dinosaur Division

81 ÷ 9

 Extra Practice Math Centers: Multiplication, Division, & More © 2007 by Mary Peterson, Scholastic Teaching Resources

Who's Missing?

Directions:

1. Players place their markers on Start.

2. Players take turns drawing a card. They decide which multiplication/division fact family member is missing from the house on the card. Answers can be checked by using the Fact Families Answer Sheet on page 78.

3. If the answer is correct, the player spins a number and moves that number of spaces on the game board. If the answer is incorrect, the next player takes a turn. The first player to reach the house is the winner.

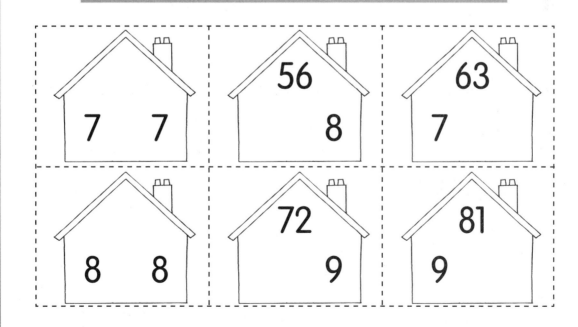

Fact Families Answer Sheet

2	3	4	5	6	7	8	9
4 (2 2)	9 (3 3)	16 (4 4)	25 (5 5)	36 (6 6)	49 (7 7)	64 (8 8)	81 (9 9)
6 (2 3)	12 (3 4)	20 (4 5)	30 (5 6)	42 (6 7)	56 (7 8)	72 (8 9)	
8 (2 4)	15 (3 5)	24 (4 6)	35 (5 7)	48 (6 8)	63 (7 9)		
10 (2 5)	18 (3 6)	28 (4 7)	40 (5 8)	54 (6 9)			
12 (2 6)	21 (3 7)	32 (4 8)	45 (5 9)				
14 (2 7)	24 (3 8)	36 (4 9)					
16 (2 8)	27 (3 9)						
18 (2 9)							

Extra Practice Math Centers: Multiplication, Division, & More © 2007 by Mary Peterson, Scholastic Teaching Resources

Who's

Start

Go ahead 4.

Go back to Start.

Go back to Start.

Go ahead 3.

Go ahead 3.

Go back 2.

Missing?

Go
back
5.

1   2
3   4

Go
ahead
2.

Go
back
5.

Go
ahead
4.

Go
ahead
3.

Extra Practice Math Centers: Multiplication, Division, & More © 2007 by Mary Peterson, Scholastic Teaching Resources

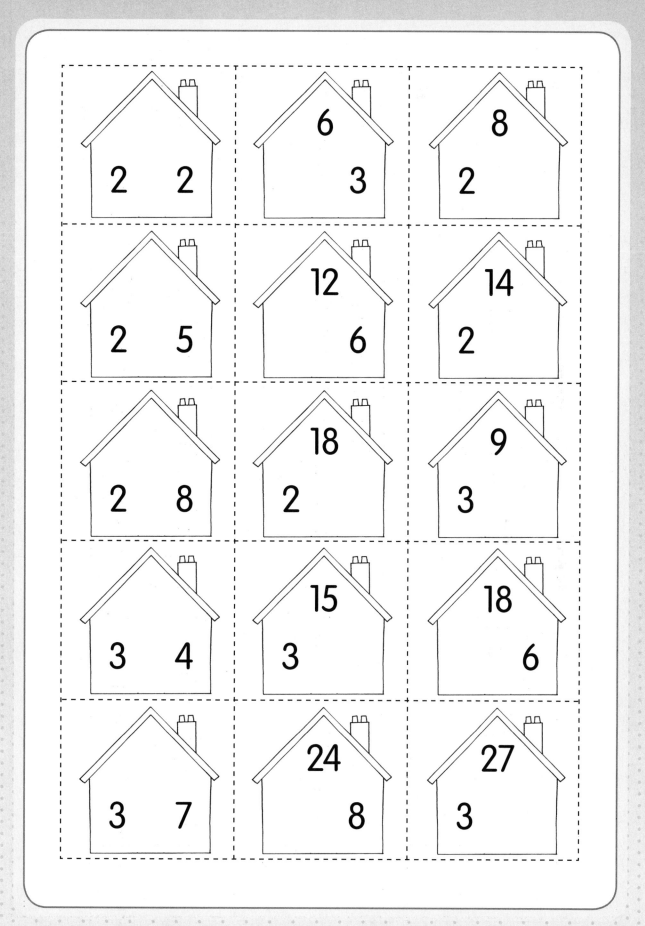

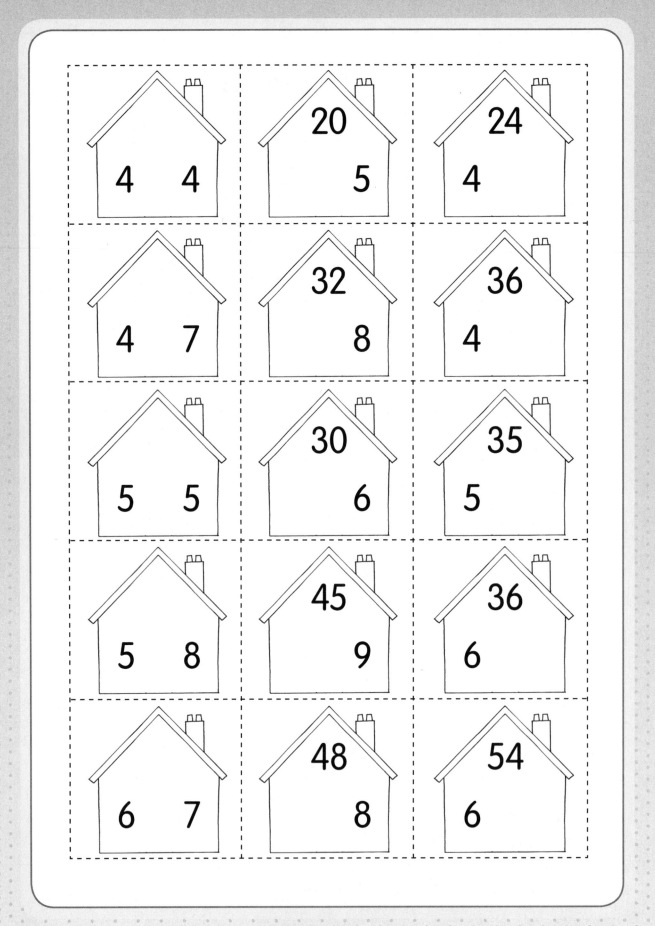

Division Swat!

Directions:

1. Players shuffle the game cards and then stack them facedown.

2. One player spins the spinner. The number the spinner lands on will be the quotient.

3. All players take turns flipping over the game cards one at a time to form another pile. When the division expression on the card matches the quotient on the spinner, players swat the card with their hands. The first player to swat keeps all the cards in the faceup pile.

4. If a player swats the wrong card, he or she must put all the cards won previously back into the facedown pile.

5. Repeat steps 2–4. Play continues until all the cards have been turned faceup. The winner is the player with the most cards at the end of the game.

Division Swat!

$2\overline{)4}$

Division Swat!

$2\overline{)6}$

Division Swat!

$2\overline{)8}$

Division Swat!

$2\overline{)10}$

Division Swat!

$2\overline{)12}$

Division Swat!

$2\overline{)14}$

Division Swat!

$2\overline{)16}$

Division Swat!

$2\overline{)18}$

Division Swat!

$3\overline{)6}$

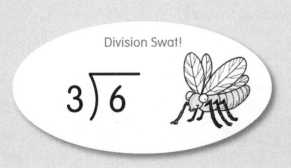

Division Swat!

$3\overline{)9}$

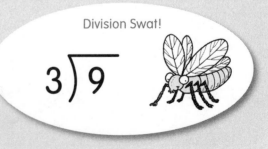

Division Swat!

12 ÷ 3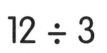

Division Swat!

15 ÷ 3

Division Swat!

18 ÷ 3

Division Swat!

21 ÷ 3

Division Swat!

24 ÷ 3

Division Swat!

27 ÷ 3

Division Swat!

8 ÷ 4

Division Swat!

12 ÷ 4

Division Swat!

16 ÷ 4

Division Swat!

20 ÷ 4

Division Swat!

4)24

Division Swat!

4)28

Division Swat!

4)32

Division Swat!

4)36

Division Swat!

5)10

Division Swat!

5)15

Division Swat!

5)20

Division Swat!

5)25

Division Swat!

5)30

Division Swat!

5)35

Division Swat!

$12 \div 6$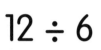

Division Swat!

$18 \div 6$

Division Swat!

$24 \div 6$

Division Swat!

$30 \div 6$

Division Swat!

$36 \div 6$

Division Swat!

$42 \div 6$

Division Swat!

$48 \div 6$

Division Swat!

$54 \div 6$

Division Swat!

$14 \div 7$

Division Swat!

$21 \div 7$

Division Swat!

$7\overline{)28}$

Division Swat!

$7\overline{)35}$

Division Swat!

$7\overline{)42}$

Division Swat!

$7\overline{)49}$

Division Swat!

$7\overline{)56}$

Division Swat!

$7\overline{)63}$

Division Swat!

$8\overline{)16}$

Division Swat!

$8\overline{)24}$

Division Swat!

$8\overline{)32}$

Division Swat!

$8\overline{)40}$

 Extra Practice Math Centers: Multiplication, Division, & More © 2007 by Mary Peterson, Scholastic Teaching Resources

Division Swat!

48 ÷ 8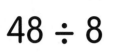

Division Swat!

56 ÷ 8

Division Swat!

64 ÷ 8

Division Swat!

72 ÷ 8

Division Swat!

18 ÷ 9

Division Swat!

27 ÷ 9

Division Swat!

36 ÷ 9

Division Swat!

45 ÷ 9

Division Swat!

54 ÷ 9

Division Swat!

63 ÷ 9

 # Divide and Go Fish

Directions:

1. Shuffle the cards and then deal four to each player. Place the remaining cards facedown in a pile.

2. The first player asks any other player if he or she holds a card that has a matching quotient. (Example: Bobby, do you have a card whose quotient equals 8?) If that player has any cards with matching quotients, he or she must give them to the player who asked.

3. The first player continues asking other players for cards. When a player does not have a matching card, that player says, "Go fish!" Then the first player takes a card from the deck. The next player takes a turn.

4. When players get all four cards with the same quotient, they have a set and place it in front of them.

5. Play continues until all cards have been collected in sets. The player with the most sets is the winner.

Sets

= 9	= 8	= 7	= 6	= 5
36 ÷ 4	56 ÷ 7	49 ÷ 7	36 ÷ 6	25 ÷ 5
81 ÷ 9	32 ÷ 4	42 ÷ 6	12 ÷ 2	10 ÷ 2
72 ÷ 8	40 ÷ 5	21 ÷ 3	30 ÷ 5	45 ÷ 9
54 ÷ 6	64 ÷ 8	63 ÷ 9	24 ÷ 4	35 ÷ 7
= 4	**= 3**	**= 2**	**= 1**	
16 ÷ 4	9 ÷ 3	4 ÷ 2	2 ÷ 2	
28 ÷ 7	18 ÷ 6	6 ÷ 3	3 ÷ 3	
12 ÷ 3	27 ÷ 9	16 ÷ 8	4 ÷ 4	
20 ÷ 5	6 ÷ 2	18 ÷ 9	5 ÷ 5	

  Extra Practice Math Centers: Multiplication, Division, & More © 2007 by Mary Peterson, Scholastic Teaching Resources

Divide and Go Fish

36 ÷ 4

Divide and Go Fish

81 ÷ 9

Divide and Go Fish

72 ÷ 8

Divide and Go Fish

54 ÷ 6

Divide and Go Fish

56 ÷ 7

Divide and Go Fish

32 ÷ 4

Divide and Go Fish

40 ÷ 5

Divide and Go Fish

64 ÷ 8

Divide and Go Fish

49 ÷ 7

Divide and Go Fish

42 ÷ 6

Divide and Go Fish
21 ÷ 3

Divide and Go Fish
63 ÷ 9

Divide and Go Fish
36 ÷ 6

Divide and Go Fish
12 ÷ 2

Divide and Go Fish
24 ÷ 4

Divide and Go Fish
30 ÷ 5

Divide and Go Fish
25 ÷ 5

Divide and Go Fish
10 ÷ 2

Divide and Go Fish
45 ÷ 9

Divide and Go Fish
35 ÷ 7

Extra Practice Math Centers: Multiplication, Division, & More © 2007 by Mary Peterson, Scholastic Teaching Resources

Divide and Go Fish

16 ÷ 4

Divide and Go Fish

28 ÷ 7

Divide and Go Fish

12 ÷ 3

Divide and Go Fish

20 ÷ 5

Divide and Go Fish

9 ÷ 3

Divide and Go Fish

18 ÷ 6

Divide and Go Fish

27 ÷ 9

Divide and Go Fish

6 ÷ 2

Divide and Go Fish

4 ÷ 2

Divide and Go Fish

6 ÷ 3

Divide and Go Fish

$16 \div 8$

Divide and Go Fish

$18 \div 9$

Divide and Go Fish

$2 \div 2$

Divide and Go Fish

$3 \div 3$

Divide and Go Fish

$4 \div 4$

Divide and Go Fish

$5 \div 5$

Division Puzzles

Directions:

1. For each puzzle, make a two-sided copy with the picture puzzle on one side and the answer cards on the other side. Cut apart the answer cards. (Note: Copy each puzzle onto a different color of card stock.)

2. The page that shows the corresponding division expressions is the game board (pp. 96, 99, 102).

3. Students read a division expression on the game board. Then they cover it with the correct answer card.

4. When answer cards cover the entire game board, students turn over the cards. If the picture puzzle is put together correctly, all the quotients are correct. If the puzzle is not put together correctly, have students check the multiplication/division grid below to find the correct quotients.

x	1	2	3	4	5	6	7	8	9
1	1	2	3	4	5	6	7	8	9
2	2	4	6	8	10	12	14	16	18
3	3	6	9	12	15	18	21	24	27
4	4	8	12	16	20	24	28	32	36
5	5	10	15	20	25	30	35	40	45
6	6	12	18	24	30	36	42	48	54
7	7	14	21	28	35	42	49	56	63
8	8	16	24	32	40	48	56	64	72
9	9	18	27	36	45	54	63	72	81

Division Puzzle 1 Game Board

Division Puzzle 1 $3\overline{)3}$	Division Puzzle 1 $2\overline{)13}$	Division Puzzle 1 $9\overline{)45}$
Division Puzzle 1 $9\overline{)10}$	Division Puzzle 1 $6\overline{)12}$	Division Puzzle 1 $2\overline{)8}$
Division Puzzle 1 $2\overline{)5}$	Division Puzzle 1 $3\overline{)9}$	Division Puzzle 1 $6\overline{)25}$
Division Puzzle 1 $2\overline{)14}$	Division Puzzle 1 $9\overline{)29}$	Division Puzzle 1 $4\overline{)32}$
Division Puzzle 1 $9\overline{)54}$	Division Puzzle 1 $8\overline{)72}$	Division Puzzle 1 $5\overline{)34}$

Division Puzzle 1 Answer Cards

Division
Puzzle 1

5

Division
Puzzle 1

6 r1

Division
Puzzle 1

1

Division
Puzzle 1

4

Division
Puzzle 1

2

Division
Puzzle 1

1 r1

Division
Puzzle 1

4 r1

Division
Puzzle 1

3

Division
Puzzle 1

2 r1

Division
Puzzle 1

8

Division
Puzzle 1

3 r2

Division
Puzzle 1

7

Division
Puzzle 1

6 r4

Division
Puzzle 1

9

Division
Puzzle 1

6

Extra Practice Math Centers: Multiplication, Division, & More © 2007 by Mary Peterson, Scholastic Teaching Resources

Division Puzzle 2 Game Board

Division Puzzle 2 $7\overline{)56}$	Division Puzzle 2 $6\overline{)50}$	Division Puzzle 2 $9\overline{)81}$
Division Puzzle 2 $7\overline{)52}$	Division Puzzle 2 $3\overline{)18}$	Division Puzzle 2 $6\overline{)37}$
Division Puzzle 2 $5\overline{)25}$	Division Puzzle 2 $5\overline{)35}$	Division Puzzle 2 $4\overline{)10}$
Division Puzzle 2 $8\overline{)24}$	Division Puzzle 2 $8\overline{)8}$	Division Puzzle 2 $3\overline{)11}$
Division Puzzle 2 $5\overline{)26}$	Division Puzzle 2 $7\overline{)14}$	Division Puzzle 2 $4\overline{)16}$

Division Puzzle 2 Answer Cards

Division Puzzle 2 **9**	Division Puzzle 2 **8 r2**	Division Puzzle 2 **8**
Division Puzzle 2 **6 r1**	Division Puzzle 2 **6**	Division Puzzle 2 **7 r3**
Division Puzzle 2 **2 r2**	Division Puzzle 2 **7**	Division Puzzle 2 **5**
Division Puzzle 2 **3 r2**	Division Puzzle 2 **1**	Division Puzzle 2 **3**
Division Puzzle 2 **4**	Division Puzzle 2 **2**	Division Puzzle 2 **5 r1**

Extra Practice Math Centers: Multiplication, Division, & More © 2007 by Mary Peterson, Scholastic Teaching Resources

Division Puzzle 3 Game Board

Division Puzzle 3 $3\overline{)15}$	Division Puzzle 3 $8\overline{)9}$	Division Puzzle 3 $8\overline{)24}$
Division Puzzle 3 $3\overline{)24}$	Division Puzzle 3 $6\overline{)36}$	Division Puzzle 3 $8\overline{)34}$
Division Puzzle 3 $7\overline{)28}$	Division Puzzle 3 $8\overline{)68}$	Division Puzzle 3 $7\overline{)49}$
Division Puzzle 3 $3\overline{)27}$	Division Puzzle 3 $3\overline{)7}$	Division Puzzle 3 $9\overline{)82}$
Division Puzzle 3 $3\overline{)18}$	Division Puzzle 3 $8\overline{)16}$	Division Puzzle 3 $9\overline{)9}$

 Extra Practice Math Centers: Multiplication, Division, & More © 2007 by Mary Peterson, Scholastic Teaching Resources

Division Puzzle 3 Answer Cards

Division Puzzle 3 3	Division Puzzle 3 1 r1	Division Puzzle 3 5
Division Puzzle 3 4 r2	Division Puzzle 3 6	Division Puzzle 3 8
Division Puzzle 3 7	Division Puzzle 3 8 r4	Division Puzzle 3 4
Division Puzzle 3 9 r1	Division Puzzle 3 2 r1	Division Puzzle 3 9
Division Puzzle 3 1	Division Puzzle 3 2	Division Puzzle 3 6

Extra Practice Math Centers: Multiplication, Division, & More © 2007 by Mary Peterson, Scholastic Teaching Resources

Division Triominoes

Directions:

1. Cut out the triominoes. Each player takes six triominoes. The player who has the triomino with all 10s will place it on the table. If no one has all 10s, the next in line is all 9s, all 8s, and so on.

2. The next player will put down one triomino, lining up the edge to match a division expression with a quotient or a quotient with a division expression. Players can check their answers on the multiplication/division grid.

3. If a player does not have a matching triomino, he or she draws another triomino and loses the turn.

4. The first player to lay down all of his or her triominoes is the winner.

X	1	2	3	4	5	6	7	8	9
1	1	2	3	4	5	6	7	8	9
2	2	4	6	8	10	12	14	16	18
3	3	6	9	12	15	18	21	24	27
4	4	8	12	16	20	24	28	32	36
5	5	10	15	20	25	30	35	40	45
6	6	12	18	24	30	36	42	48	54
7	7	14	21	28	35	42	49	56	63
8	8	16	24	32	40	48	56	64	72
9	9	18	27	36	45	54	63	72	81

Division Triominoes

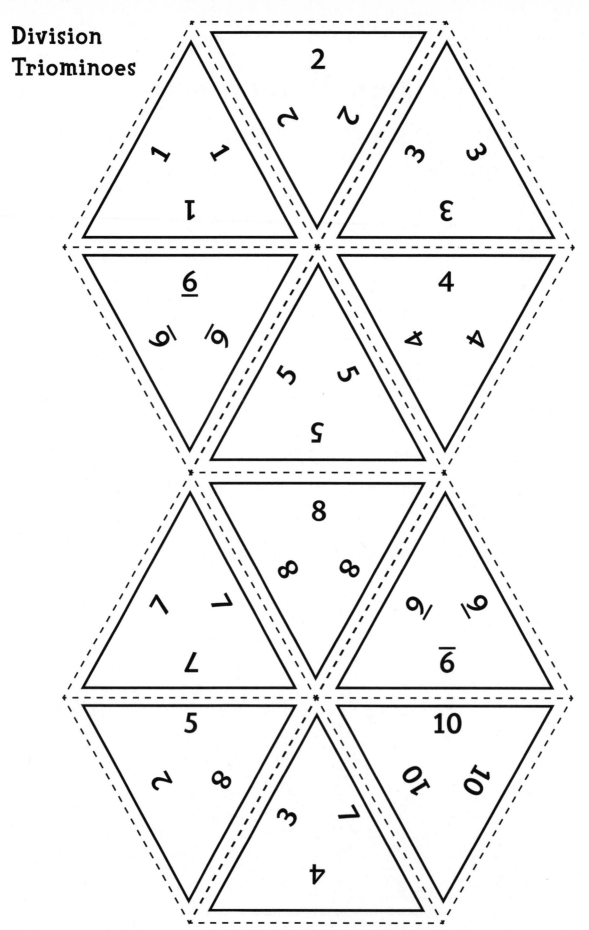

Extra Practice Math Centers: Multiplication, Division, & More © 2007 by Mary Peterson, Scholastic Teaching Resources

Division
Triominoes

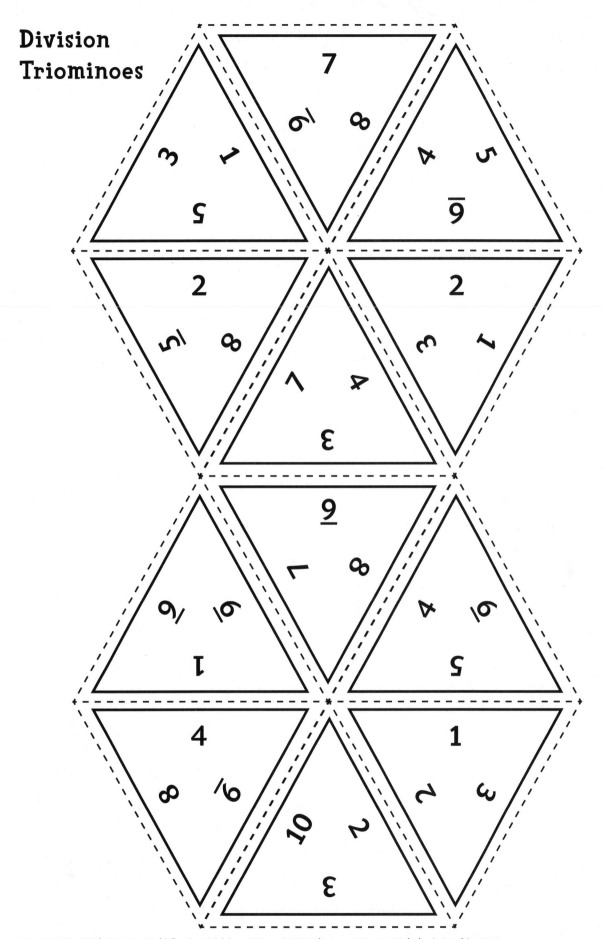

Division Triominoes

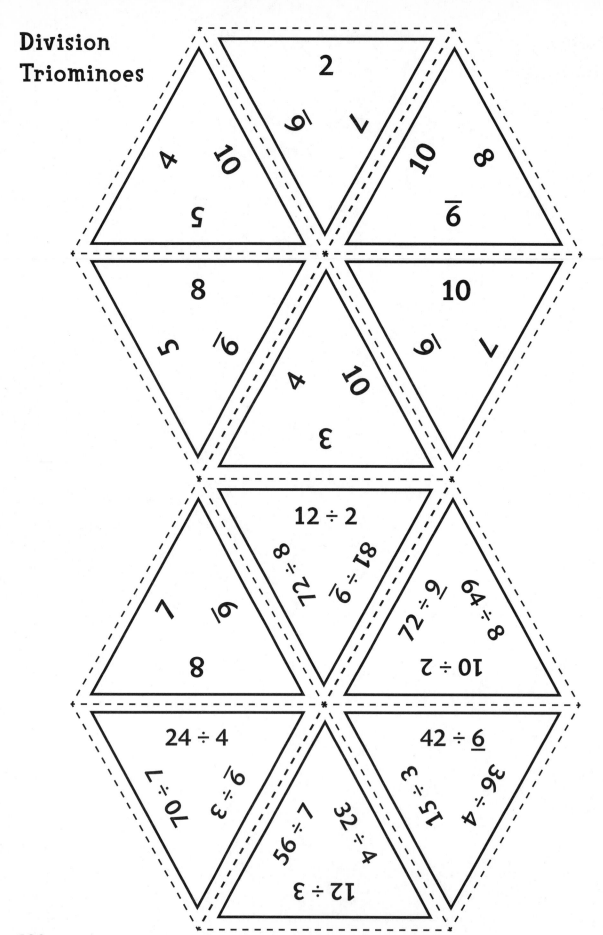

Division Triominoes

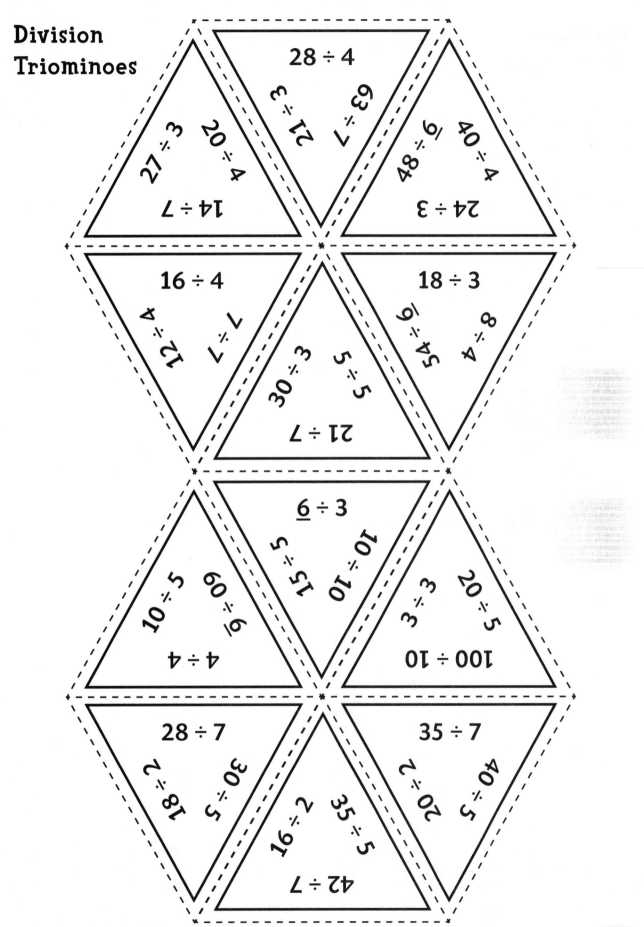

Division Triominoes

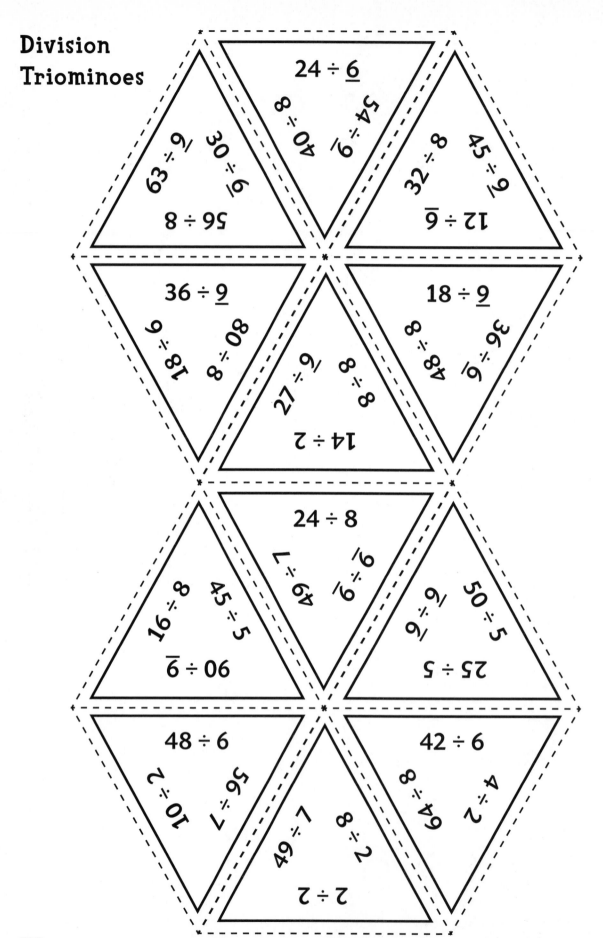

Extra Practice Math Centers: Multiplication, Division, & More © 2007 by Mary Peterson, Scholastic Teaching Resources

Fraction
Centers

Board Games

....

Card Games

....

Bingo

....

Take the Cake

Directions:

1. Players place their markers on the cake. They take turns drawing a game card and solving the fraction problem on it. Players can use the answer card below to check answers.

2. If the answer is correct, the player spins and moves his or her marker that number of spaces around the game board.

3. The first player to go all the way around the game board and return to the cake is the winner.

Answer Card

1. $1\frac{1}{2}$ cups	**11.** 7 cookies	**21.** 4 cupcakes
2. $\frac{1}{2}$	**12.** 21 cookies	**22.** 8 cupcakes
3. 6 eggs	**13.** $\frac{1}{3}$ cup	**23.** 12 cupcakes
4. $\frac{1}{4}$ cup	**14.** $\frac{1}{3}$	**24.** $1\frac{1}{2}$ cups
5. $\frac{3}{8}$	**15.** $\frac{4}{10}$ or $\frac{2}{5}$	**25.** 3 pieces
6. 45 minutes	**16.** $\frac{1}{6}$	**26.** 75 minutes
7. 18 cupcakes	**17.** 21 cupcakes	**27.** 27 cakes
8. $\frac{1}{6}$ pound	**18.** $\frac{1}{2}$	**28.** $\frac{1}{3}$
9. 4 spoonfuls	**19.** 10 half cups	**29.** 4
10. $\frac{1}{3}$	**20.** $\frac{1}{2}$	**30.** $\frac{1}{6}$

 Extra Practice Math Centers: Multiplication, Division, & More © 2007 by Mary Peterson, Scholastic Teaching Resources

			Go back 2 spaces.		Lose a turn.

Take

Go ahead 3 spaces.

Lose a turn.

Go back to Start.

Start

Finish

Lose a turn.

the Cake

		Go ahead 3 spaces.			

Take another turn.

Go back 2 spaces.

1	2
3	4

Take another turn.			Lose a turn.		

Take the Cake

1. A cookie recipe calls for $\frac{3}{4}$ cups of sugar. You double the recipe. How much sugar should you use?

Take the Cake

2. Dan cut the cake into 6 equal pieces. Three children each had one piece. Dan ate the rest. What fraction of the cake did Dan eat?

Take the Cake

3. John needs $\frac{1}{2}$ dozen eggs to make cookies. How many eggs does he need?

Take the Cake

4. A recipe calls for $\frac{3}{4}$ cup of flour. Bob already added $\frac{1}{2}$ cup. How much more flour does he need to add?

Take the Cake

5. A cake is cut into 8 equal pieces. Maria eats $\frac{1}{4}$, and John eats $\frac{3}{8}$ of the cake. How much cake is left?

Take the Cake

6. A chocolate cake needs to bake for $\frac{3}{4}$ of an hour. How many minutes does it need to bake?

Take the Cake

7. Susan makes 45 cupcakes. She takes $\frac{2}{5}$ of them to a party at school. How many cupcakes does Susan take to school?

Take the Cake

8. The children need 1 pound of flour to make bread. Mark bought $\frac{1}{3}$ pound. Joe bought $\frac{1}{2}$ pound. How much more flour do they need?

Take the Cake

9. A cake recipe calls for 1 teaspoon of salt. Leah only has a $\frac{1}{4}$ teaspoon measure. How many $\frac{1}{4}$ teaspoons of salt should she put in the cake?

Take the Cake

10. Mrs. Jones bought 30 cupcakes: 10 chocolate, 15 vanilla, and 5 spice. What fraction are chocolate?

Take the Cake

11. Mr. Bill has a bag of 28 cookies. Half are chocolate, $\frac{1}{4}$ are sugar, and the rest are oatmeal. How many oatmeal cookies are there?

Take the Cake

12. Mr. Bill has a bag of 28 cookies. Half are chocolate, $\frac{1}{4}$ are sugar, and the rest are oatmeal. What is the total number of chocolate and sugar cookies?

Take the Cake

13. A recipe calls for 1 cup of oatmeal. Sally adds $\frac{1}{3}$ cup. Ben adds $\frac{1}{3}$ cup. How much more oatmeal do they need?

Take the Cake

14. Pete puts 3 gumdrops on a cake. Sal puts on 9, and Larry puts on 6. What fraction of gumdrops does Larry put on the cake?

Take the Cake

15. A cake is cut into 10 equal pieces. Sam eats 4 pieces. What fraction of the cake does Sam eat?

Take the Cake

16. Pete puts 3 gumdrops on a cake. Sal puts on 9, and Larry puts on 6. What fraction of gumdrops does Pete put on the cake?

Take the Cake

17. Molly bakes 56 cupcakes. She gives $\frac{3}{8}$ of them to her sister. How many cupcakes does Molly give to her sister?

Take the Cake

18. Pete puts 3 gumdrops on a cake. Sal puts on 9, and Larry puts on 6. What fraction of gumdrops does Sal put on the cake?

Take the Cake

19. A cake recipe calls for 5 cups of flour. Al only has a $\frac{1}{2}$-cup measure. How many $\frac{1}{2}$ cups of flour should he use?

Take the Cake

20. A cake is cut into 14 equal pieces. Casey eats 7 pieces of the cake. What fraction of the cake does he eat?

 Extra Practice Math Centers: Multiplication, Division, & More © 2007 by Mary Peterson, Scholastic Teaching Resources

Take the Cake

21. Ray has 32 cupcakes. He eats $\frac{1}{2}$ of them. Bob eats $\frac{1}{4}$, and Jim eats $\frac{1}{8}$. How many cupcakes are left?

Take the Cake

22. Ray has 32 cupcakes. He eats $\frac{1}{2}$ of them. Bob eats $\frac{1}{4}$, and Jim eats $\frac{1}{8}$. How many more cupcakes does Ray eat than Bob?

Take the Cake

23. Ray has 32 cupcakes. He eats $\frac{1}{2}$ of them. Bob eats $\frac{1}{4}$, and Jim eats $\frac{1}{8}$. How many cupcakes do Bob and Jim eat all together?

Take the Cake

24. A recipe calls for $2\frac{1}{4}$ cups of flour. Nancy has added $\frac{3}{4}$ cup. How much more flour does she need to add?

Take the Cake

25. A cake is cut into 12 equal pieces. Mario eats $\frac{1}{6}$, Joe eats $\frac{1}{4}$, and Sally eats $\frac{1}{3}$ of the cake. How many pieces are left?

Take the Cake

26. A cake needs to bake at 400° for $\frac{3}{4}$ of an hour. Then it needs to bake for another $\frac{1}{2}$ hour at 300°. How many minutes does the cake bake?

Take the Cake

27. Sandy buys 36 cakes. She takes $\frac{3}{4}$ of them to school. How many cakes does Sandy take to school?

Take the Cake

28. Mrs. Hall puts 24 gumdrops on a cake: 12 red, 4 yellow, and 8 orange. What fraction of the gumdrops are orange?

Take the Cake

29. A cake recipe calls for 3 cups of flour. Julia only has a $\frac{3}{4}$-cup measure. How many $\frac{3}{4}$ cups of flour should she use?

Take the Cake

30. Mrs. Hall puts 24 gumdrops on a cake: 12 red, 4 yellow, and 8 orange. What fraction of the gumdrops are yellow?

Super Shopper

Directions:

1. Players place their markers on the shopping cart.

2. They take turns drawing a shopping card. Then they must use the discount on the card to find the sale price.

3. Players use the answer card below to check answers. If the answer is correct, the player keeps the card. Then the player spins to see how many spaces he or she gets to move. If it's incorrect, the player returns the card to the bottom of the pile.

4. When all players have the reached the cash register, they add the sale prices of all their shopping cards. Whoever has the highest total is the winner.

Answer Card

1.	$10.00	**11.**	$1.25	**21.**	$14.85
2.	$14.00	**12.**	$2.00	**22.**	$2.00
3.	$3.00	**13.**	$0.60	**23.**	$16.00
4.	$63.00	**14.**	$7.50	**24.**	$28.00
5.	$3.75	**15.**	$20.00	**25.**	$5.00
6.	$3.80	**16.**	$3.50	**26.**	$4.40
7.	$111.00	**17.**	$5.00	**27.**	$12.50
8.	$4.00	**18.**	$4.00	**28.**	$49.00
9.	$15.00	**19.**	$56.00	**29.**	$14.00
10.	$6.00	**20.**	$80.00	**30.**	$12.00

Extra Practice Math Centers: Multiplication, Division, & More © 2007 by Mary Peterson, Scholastic Teaching Resources

	Go back 2 spaces.			Lose a turn.	

Super

Go ahead 2 spaces.					

Lose a turn.		Take another turn.		Go back to Start.	
		Go back to Start.			
Start				Lose a turn.	

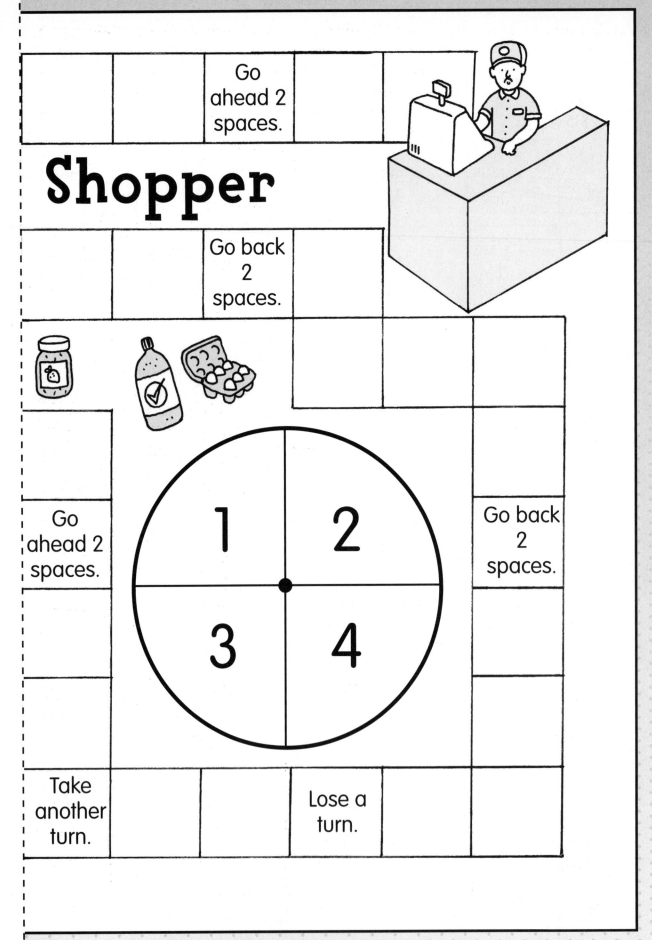

Go ahead 2 spaces.

Shopper

Go back 2 spaces.

Go ahead 2 spaces.

1 2

3 4

Go back 2 spaces.

Take another turn.

Lose a turn.

Extra Practice Math Centers: Multiplication, Division, & More © 2007 by Mary Peterson, Scholastic Teaching Resources

Super Shopper

1. soccer ball
$15.00

$\frac{1}{3}$ off

Super Shopper

2. skateboard
$28.00

$\frac{1}{2}$ off

Super Shopper

3. football
$12.00

$\frac{3}{4}$ off

Super Shopper

4. canoe and paddle $84.00

$\frac{1}{4}$ off

Super Shopper

5. dictionary
$5.00

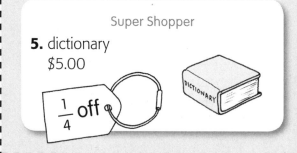

$\frac{1}{4}$ off

Super Shopper

6. dartboard with dart
$4.75

$\frac{1}{5}$ off

Super Shopper

7. desktop computer
$333.00

$\frac{2}{3}$ off

Super Shopper

8. pencil sharpener
$6.00

$\frac{1}{3}$ off

Super Shopper

9. umbrella
$18.00

$\frac{1}{6}$ off

Super Shopper

10. horn
$12.00

$\frac{1}{2}$ off

Super Shopper

11. yo-yo
$2.50

$\frac{1}{2}$ off

Super Shopper

12. scooter
$5.00

$\frac{3}{5}$ off

Super Shopper

13. box of crayons
$0.90

$\frac{1}{3}$ off

Super Shopper

14. teddy bear
$10.00

$\frac{1}{4}$ off

Super Shopper

15. portable radio
$25.00

$\frac{1}{5}$ off

Super Shopper

16. kite
$4.00

$\frac{1}{8}$ off

Super Shopper

17. walkman with headphones
$15.00

$\frac{2}{3}$ off

Super Shopper

18. calculator with batteries
$10.00

$\frac{3}{5}$ off

Super Shopper

19. computer game
$64.00

$\frac{1}{8}$ off

Super Shopper

20. TV
$96.00

$\frac{1}{6}$ off

Super Shopper

21. backpack
$16.50

$\frac{1}{10}$ off

Super Shopper

22. baseball cap
$8.00

$\frac{3}{4}$ off

Super Shopper

23. shirt
$20.00

$\frac{2}{10}$ off

Super Shopper

24. jacket
$40.00

$\frac{3}{10}$ off

Super Shopper

25. sun visor
$7.50

$\frac{1}{3}$ off

Super Shopper

26. pair of mittens
$5.50

$\frac{1}{5}$ off

Super Shopper

27. pair of tennis shoes
$25.00

$\frac{1}{2}$ off

Super Shopper

28. bicycle
$98.00

$\frac{1}{2}$ off

Super Shopper

29. tricycle
$35.00

$\frac{3}{5}$ off

Super Shopper

30. baseball and bat
$16.00

$\frac{1}{4}$ off

Measuring Concentration

Directions:

1. Spread the cards facedown on a table.

2. Players take turns turning over two cards. When a player matches two equivalent measurements, he or she keeps the cards and takes another turn. Players can use the chart of equivalent measurements below to check answers.

3. If the cards do not show equivalent measurements, the player turns them over. The next player takes a turn.

4. When all the matches have been made, the player with the most cards is the winner.

Equivalent Measurements

6 inches = $\frac{1}{2}$ foot	2 feet = $\frac{2}{3}$ yard
16 ounces = 1 pound	1,000 pounds = $\frac{1}{2}$ ton
3 feet = 1 yard	$\frac{2}{3}$ foot = 8 inches
8 ounces = $\frac{1}{2}$ pound	$\frac{1}{4}$ pound = 4 ounces
12 inches = 1 foot	2 ounces = $\frac{1}{8}$ pound
3 quarts = $\frac{3}{4}$ gallon	2 cups = 1 pint
2 quarts = $\frac{1}{2}$ gallon	16 cups = 1 gallon
1 quart = 2 pints	6 cups = 3 pints
12 eggs = 1 dozen	4 eggs = $\frac{1}{3}$ dozen
2 eggs = $\frac{1}{6}$ dozen	6 eggs = $\frac{1}{2}$ dozen

 Extra Practice Math Centers: Multiplication, Division, & More © 2007 by Mary Peterson, Scholastic Teaching Resources

 Measuring Concentration

6 inches

 Measuring Concentration

16 ounces

 Measuring Concentration

3 feet

 Measuring Concentration

8 ounces

 Measuring Concentration

2 feet

 Measuring Concentration

1,000 pounds

 Measuring Concentration

8 inches

 Measuring Concentration

4 ounces

 Measuring Concentration

12 inches

 Measuring Concentration

2 ounces

 Measuring Concentration

3 quarts

 Measuring Concentration

2 cups

 Measuring Concentration

2 quarts

 Measuring Concentration

16 cups

 Measuring Concentration

2 pints

 Measuring Concentration

6 cups

 Measuring Concentration

12 eggs

 Measuring Concentration

4 eggs

 Measuring Concentration

2 eggs

 Measuring Concentration

6 eggs

Extra Practice Math Centers: Multiplication, Division, & More © 2007 by Mary Peterson, Scholastic Teaching Resources

Measuring Concentration

$\frac{3}{4}$ gallon

Measuring Concentration

1 pint

Measuring Concentration

$\frac{1}{2}$ gallon

Measuring Concentration

1 gallon

Measuring Concentration

1 quart

Measuring Concentration

3 pints

Measuring Concentration

1 dozen

Measuring Concentration

$\frac{1}{3}$ dozen

Measuring Concentration

$\frac{1}{6}$ dozen

Measuring Concentration

$\frac{1}{2}$ dozen

 Measuring Concentration

$\frac{1}{2}$ foot

 Measuring Concentration

1 pound

 Measuring Concentration

1 yard

 Measuring Concentration

$\frac{1}{2}$ pound

 Measuring Concentration

$\frac{2}{3}$ yard

 Measuring Concentration

$\frac{1}{2}$ ton

 Measuring Concentration

$\frac{2}{3}$ foot

 Measuring Concentration

$\frac{1}{4}$ pound

 Measuring Concentration

1 foot

 Measuring Concentration

$\frac{1}{8}$ pound

Extra Practice Math Centers: Multiplication, Division, & More © 2007 by Mary Peterson, Scholastic Teaching Resources

Fraction War

Directions:

1. Shuffle the cards and place them facedown. (Note: Make two copies of the game cards on pages 130–131.)

2. Each player takes two cards. He or she places the smaller number in the top box to show a numerator and then places the larger number in the bottom box to show the denominator. The player with the greater fraction keeps both sets of cards.

3. If players are unsure which fraction is greater, they should multiply their numerator by their opponent's denominator. The greater number wins.

4. When all the cards have been drawn, the player with the most cards wins the game.

Extra Practice Math Centers: Multiplication, Division, & More © 2007 by Mary Peterson, Scholastic Teaching Resources

Fraction War 1

Fraction War 2

Fraction War 3

Fraction War 4

Fraction War 5

Fraction War 6

Fraction War 7

Fraction War 8

Fraction War 9

Fraction Boxes

Directions:

1. Cut out the fraction pieces and put them in a container. Each player takes one whole box (1) from page 133.

2. Players take turns spinning the spinner. They find the fraction in the container that matches the fraction they spin and place it on the one whole box. If there is no matching fraction in the container or if the fraction does not fit in the one whole box, they lose their turn.

3. The first player to completely cover their one whole box is the winner.

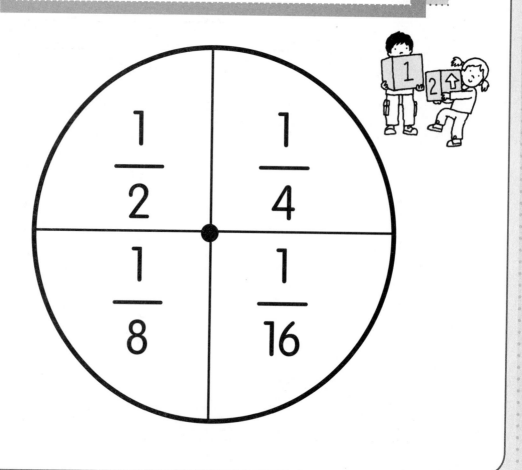

Extra Practice Math Centers: Multiplication, Division, & More © 2007 by Mary Peterson, Scholastic Teaching Resources

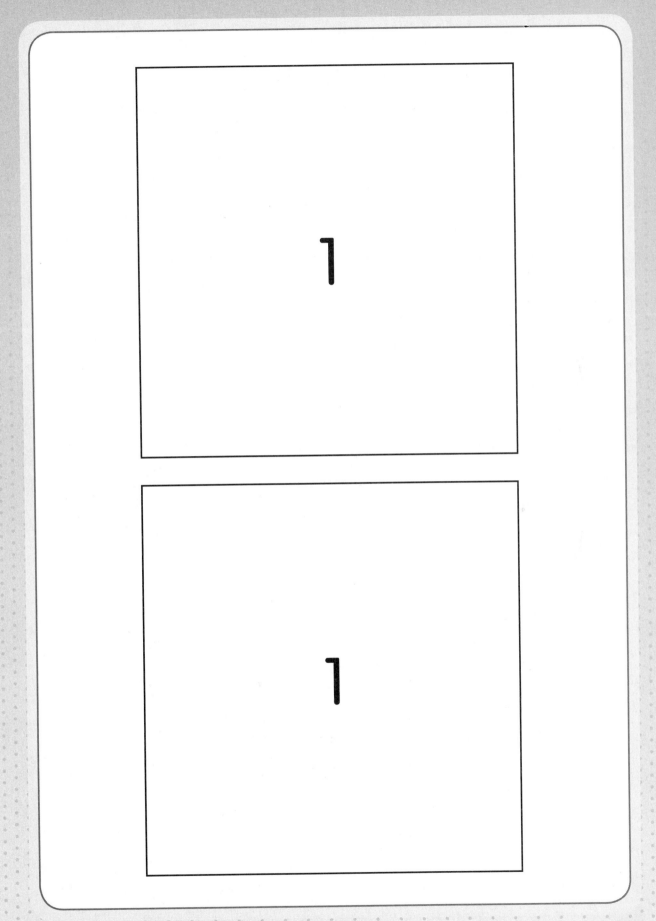

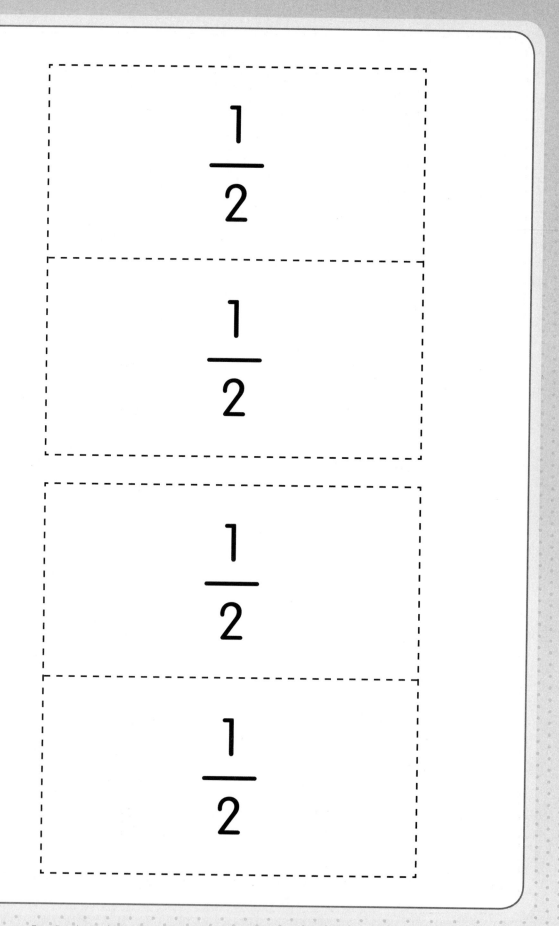

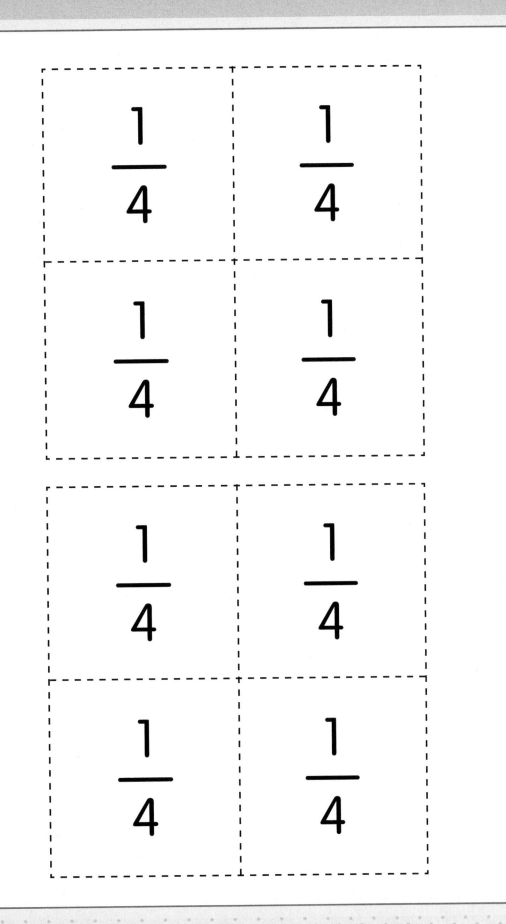

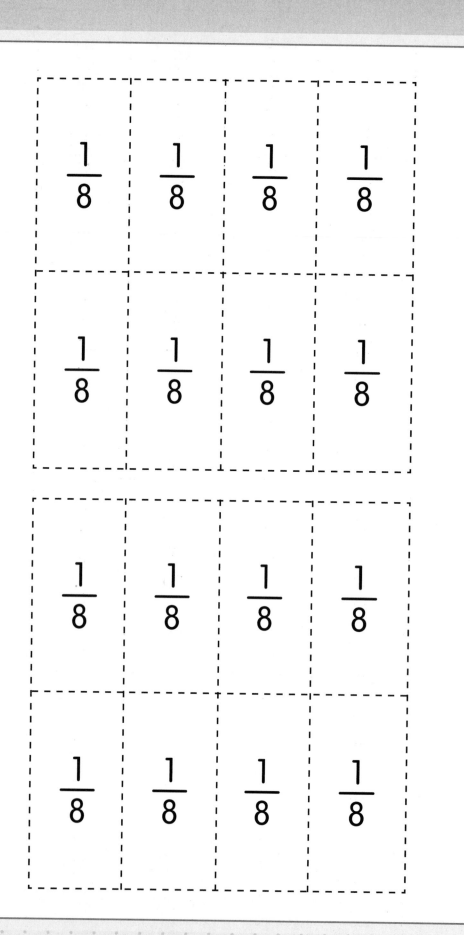

$\dfrac{1}{16}$	$\dfrac{1}{16}$	$\dfrac{1}{16}$	$\dfrac{1}{16}$
$\dfrac{1}{16}$	$\dfrac{1}{16}$	$\dfrac{1}{16}$	$\dfrac{1}{16}$
$\dfrac{1}{16}$	$\dfrac{1}{16}$	$\dfrac{1}{16}$	$\dfrac{1}{16}$
$\dfrac{1}{16}$	$\dfrac{1}{16}$	$\dfrac{1}{16}$	$\dfrac{1}{16}$
$\dfrac{1}{16}$	$\dfrac{1}{16}$	$\dfrac{1}{16}$	$\dfrac{1}{16}$
$\dfrac{1}{16}$	$\dfrac{1}{16}$	$\dfrac{1}{16}$	$\dfrac{1}{16}$
$\dfrac{1}{16}$	$\dfrac{1}{16}$	$\dfrac{1}{16}$	$\dfrac{1}{16}$
$\dfrac{1}{16}$	$\dfrac{1}{16}$	$\dfrac{1}{16}$	$\dfrac{1}{16}$

Fraction Bingo

Directions for pages 139–143:

1. Shuffle the fraction cards. Players draw one card at a time. (Note: Make as many copies of the game cards on page 139 as there are players.)

2. Each player finds that fraction model on his or her game board and covers it with the card.

3. The first player to place four cards in a row wins the game.

Directions for pages 144–148:

1. This game is more difficult. Players draw one card at a time. (Note: Make as many copies of page 144 as there are players.)

2. Each player must find the model of an equivalent fraction on the game board and cover it with the card. Players can check their answers on the Equivalent Fractions card below.

3. The first player to place four cards in a row is the winner. (**Note:** Copy the two bingo games on different colors of card stock.)

Equivalent Fractions

$\dfrac{1}{2} = \dfrac{2}{4} = \dfrac{3}{6} = \dfrac{4}{8} = \dfrac{5}{10}$		$\dfrac{1}{3} = \dfrac{2}{6} = \dfrac{3}{9}$
$\dfrac{2}{3} = \dfrac{4}{6} = \dfrac{6}{9}$		$\dfrac{1}{4} = \dfrac{2}{8}$
$\dfrac{3}{4} = \dfrac{6}{8}$		$\dfrac{1}{5} = \dfrac{2}{10}$
$\dfrac{3}{5} = \dfrac{6}{10}$		$\dfrac{4}{5} = \dfrac{8}{10}$
$\dfrac{1}{6} = \dfrac{2}{12}$		$\dfrac{5}{6} = \dfrac{10}{12}$
$\dfrac{2}{5} = \dfrac{4}{10}$		

Fraction Bingo 1
Game Cards

$\dfrac{1}{2}$	$\dfrac{1}{3}$	$\dfrac{1}{4}$	$\dfrac{1}{6}$
$\dfrac{1}{5}$	$\dfrac{7}{10}$	$\dfrac{7}{8}$	$\dfrac{2}{3}$
$\dfrac{4}{5}$	$\dfrac{3}{8}$	$\dfrac{3}{5}$	$\dfrac{2}{5}$
$\dfrac{3}{4}$	$\dfrac{5}{8}$	$\dfrac{3}{10}$	$\dfrac{5}{6}$

Fraction Bingo 1
Game Board

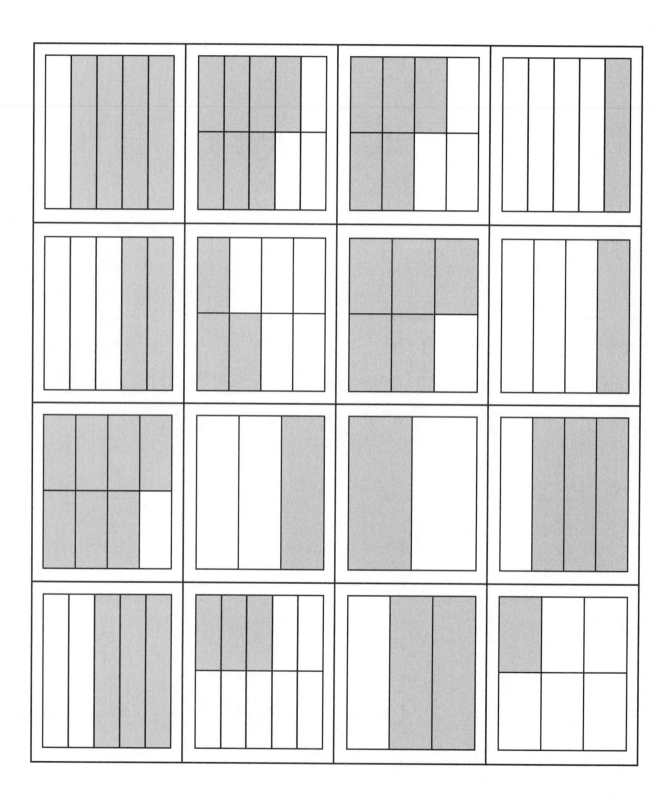

Extra Practice Math Centers: Multiplication, Division, & More © 2007 by Mary Peterson, Scholastic Teaching Resources

Fraction Bingo 1
Game Board

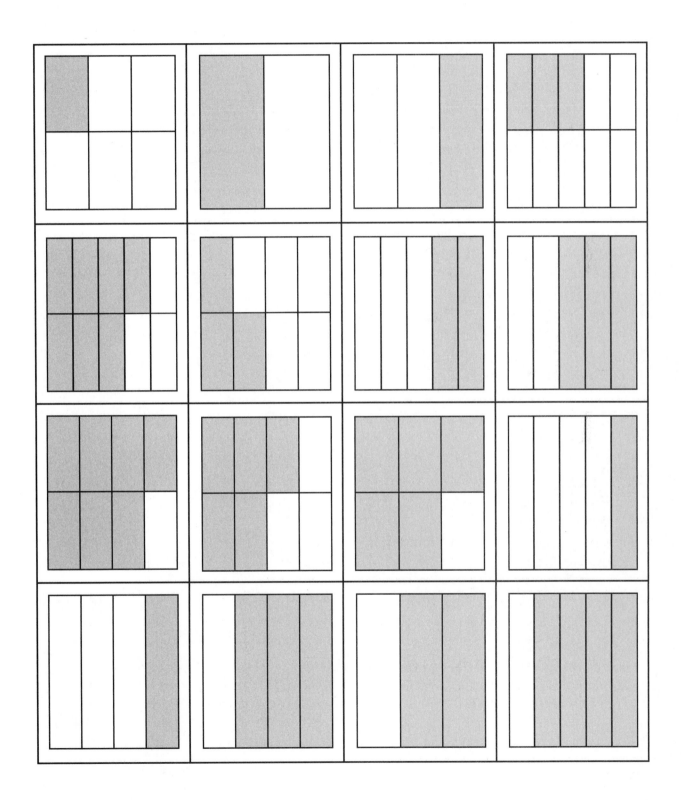

Fraction Bingo 1
Game Board

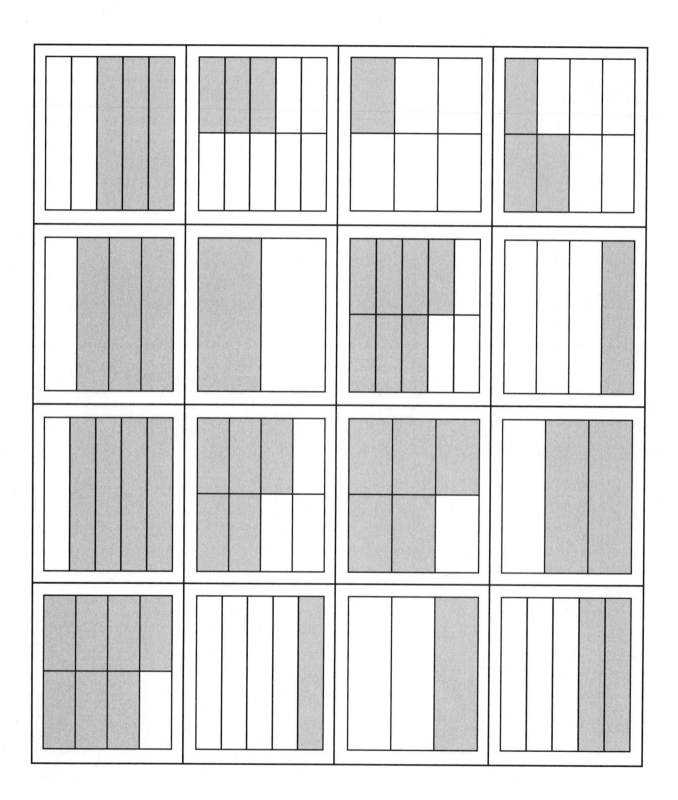

Extra Practice Math Centers: Multiplication, Division, & More © 2007 by Mary Peterson, Scholastic Teaching Resources

Fraction Bingo 1
Game Board

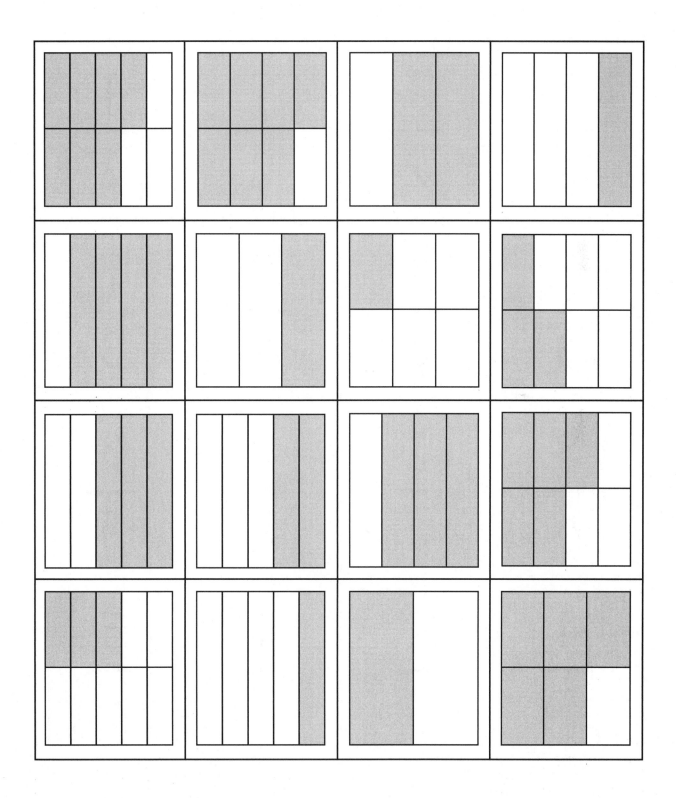

Fraction Bingo 2
Game Cards

$\dfrac{1}{2}$	$\dfrac{1}{2}$	$\dfrac{1}{2}$	$\dfrac{1}{2}$
$\dfrac{1}{3}$	$\dfrac{1}{3}$	$\dfrac{2}{3}$	$\dfrac{2}{3}$
$\dfrac{3}{4}$	$\dfrac{1}{5}$	$\dfrac{2}{5}$	$\dfrac{3}{5}$
$\dfrac{4}{5}$	$\dfrac{1}{4}$	$\dfrac{1}{6}$	$\dfrac{5}{6}$

Fraction Bingo 2
Game Board

Fraction Bingo 2
Game Board

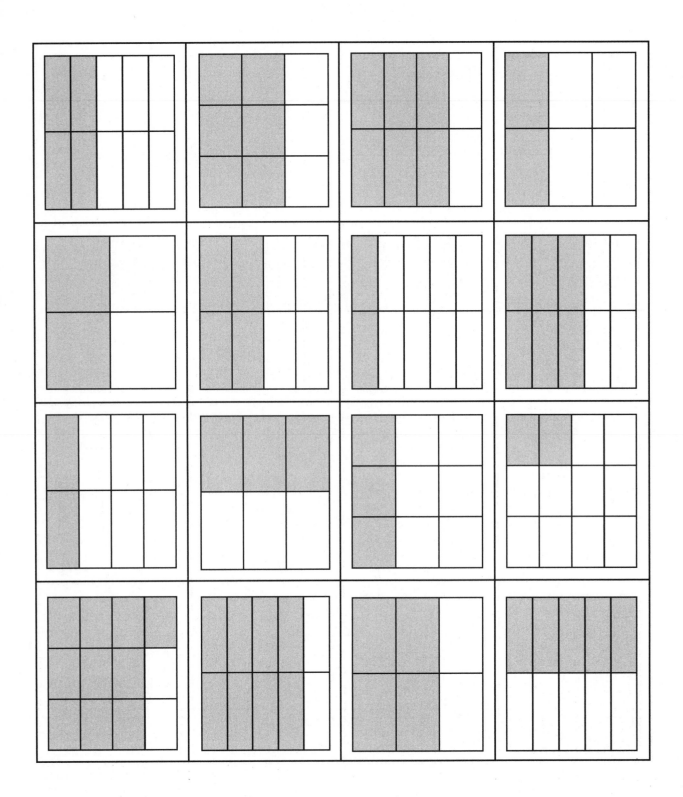

Extra Practice Math Centers: Multiplication, Division, & More © 2007 by Mary Peterson, Scholastic Teaching Resources

Fraction Bingo 2
Game Board

Fraction Bingo 2
Game Board

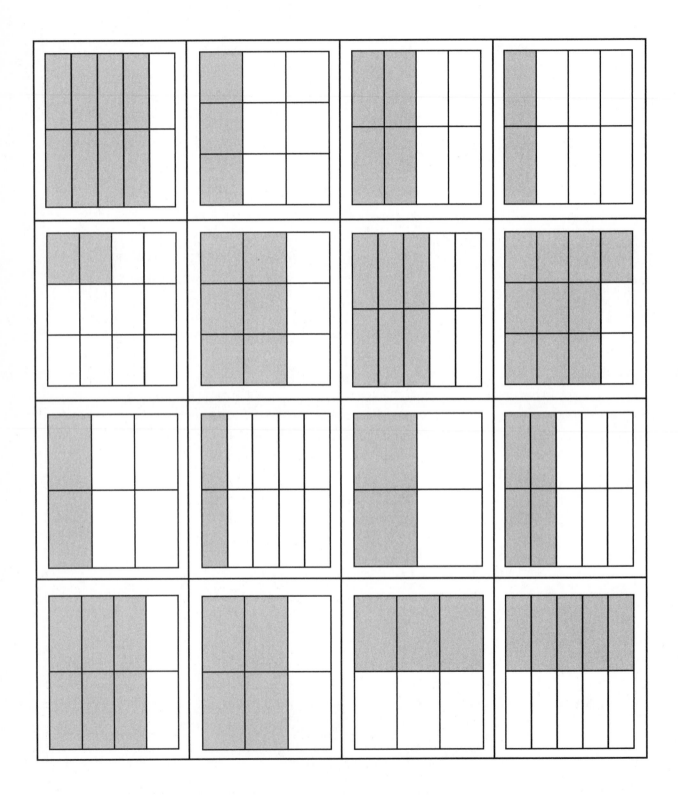

Extra Practice Math Centers: Multiplication, Division, & More © 2007 by Mary Peterson, Scholastic Teaching Resources

Pizza Party

Directions:

1. Cut the pizzas into slices, and place them in a container. Cut out the pizza pans.

2. Each player takes a pizza pan. Players take turns spinning the spinner. They find the fraction in the container that matches the fraction they spin and place it on their pizza pan. If there is no matching fraction in the container or if the fraction does not fit in the pan, they lose their turn.

3. The first player to complete a whole pizza is the winner.

Variation:

Players begin with a full pan of pizza slices. They take turns spinning to remove slices. They may take away equivalent fractions. The first player to remove all the slices is the winner.

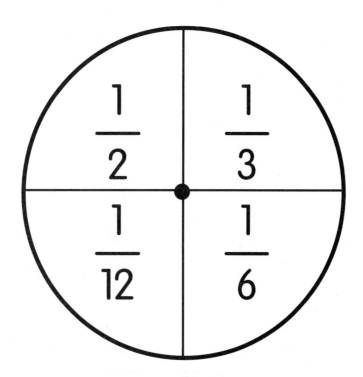

Pizza Party

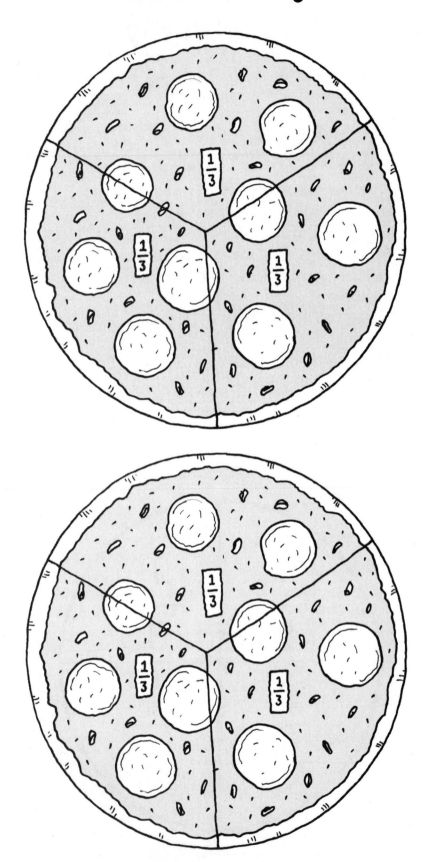

Extra Practice Math Centers: Multiplication, Division, & More © 2007 by Mary Peterson, Scholastic Teaching Resources

Pizza Party

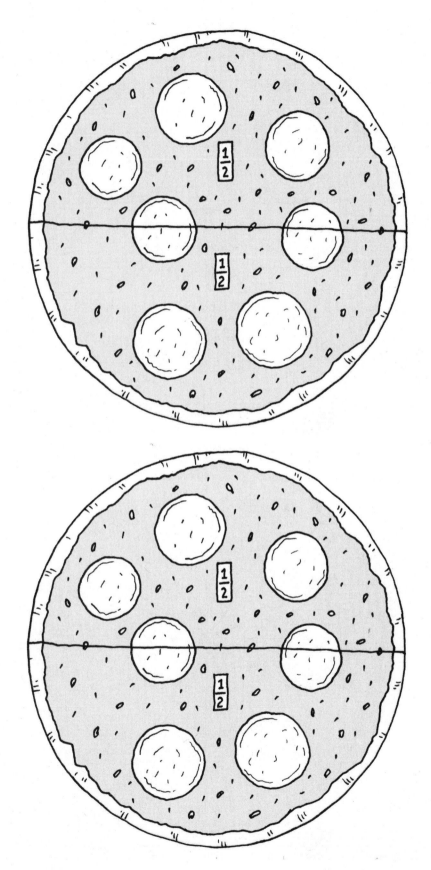

Pizza Party

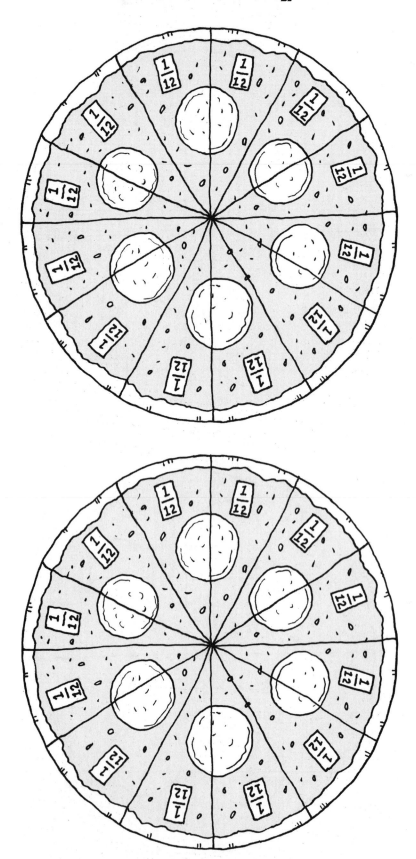

Pizza Party

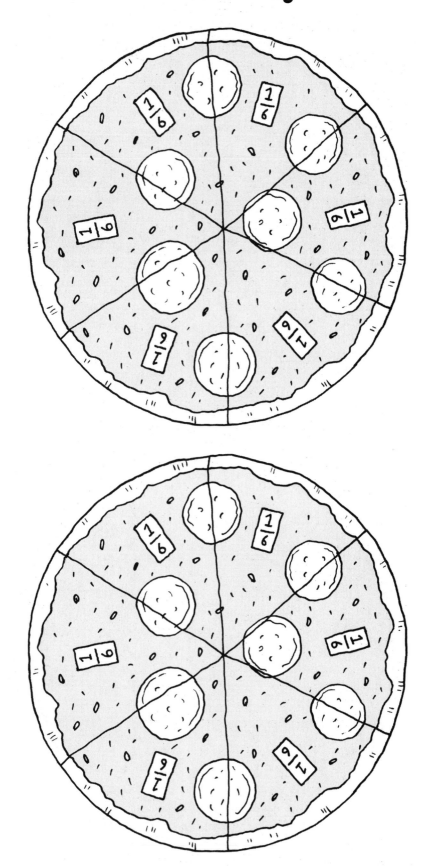

Pizza Party Pans

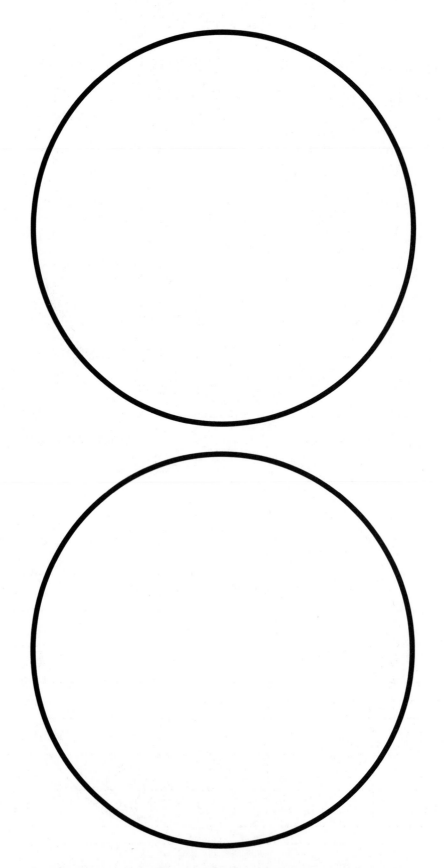

Fraction Pie

Directions:

1. Players place their game markers on Start.

2. Players take turns drawing a game card. They must solve the fraction problem on the card. An answer card is shown below. If the answer is correct, the player spins the spinner and moves that number of spaces on the game board.

3. The first player to reach the woman holding the pie is the winner.

Answer Card

A = 6	B = 8	C = 3	D = 9	E = 4
F = 2	G = 10	H = 5	I = 10	J = 3
K = 6	L = 9	M = 12	N = 8	O = 4
P = 3	Q = 6	R = 5	S = 2	T = 4
U = 6	V = 8	W = 4	X = 2	Y = 6
Z = 3	AA = 2	BB = 4	CC = 1	DD = 5
EE = 1	FF = 3	GG = 5	HH = 7	II = 2
JJ = 4	KK = 7	LL = 9	MM = 6	NN = 12
OO = 3	PP = 15	QQ = 2	RR = 8	SS = 14

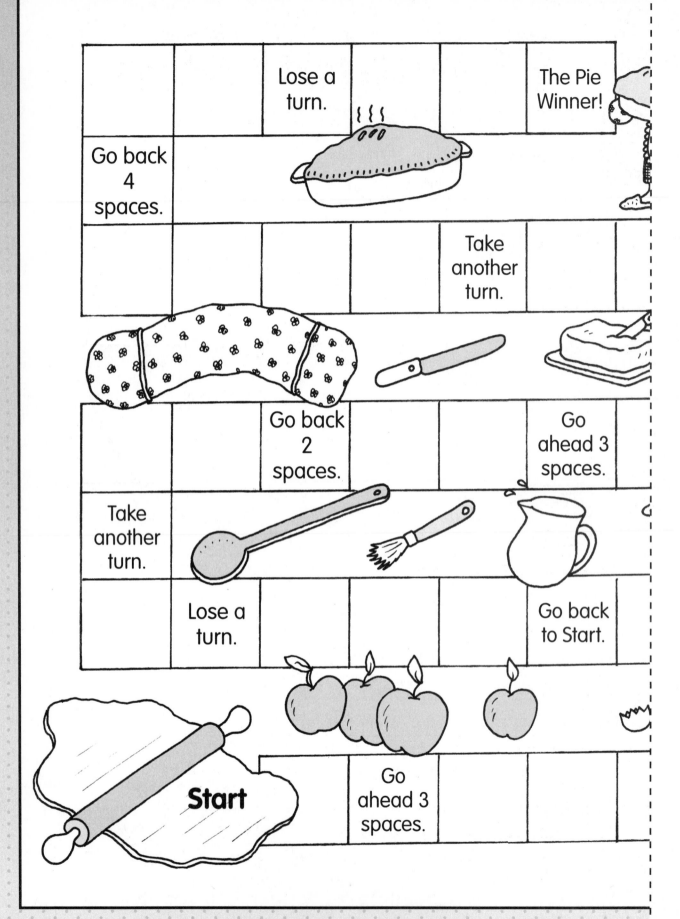

Lose a turn.

The Pie Winner!

Go back 4 spaces.

Take another turn.

Go back 2 spaces.

Go ahead 3 spaces.

Take another turn.

Lose a turn.

Go back to Start.

Start

Go ahead 3 spaces.

Fraction Pie

Go back
2
spaces.

1   2
4   3

Lose a
turn.

FLOUR

Go back
to Start.

Take
another
turn.

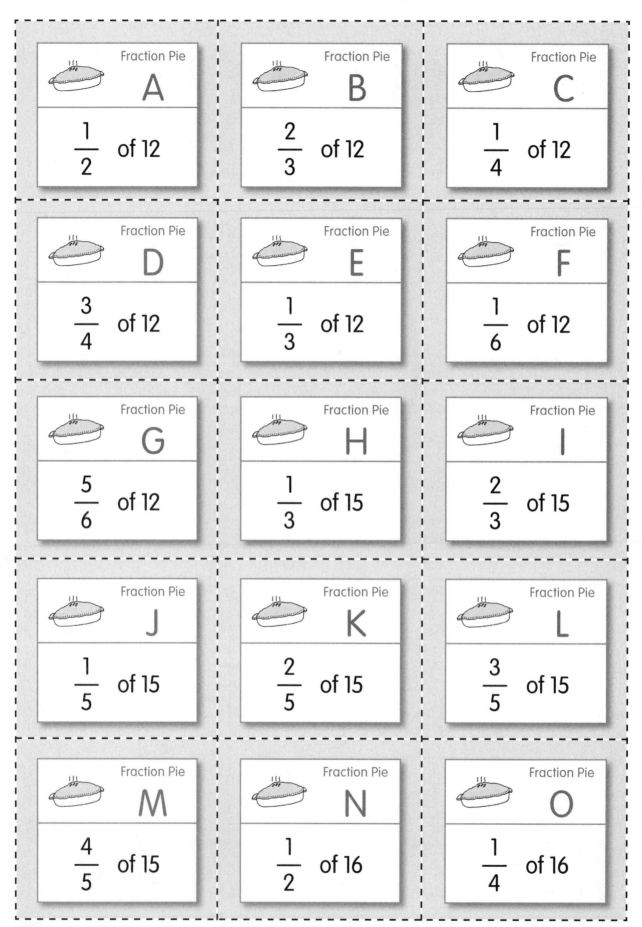

Fraction Pie **A**	Fraction Pie **B**	Fraction Pie **C**
$\frac{1}{2}$ of 12	$\frac{2}{3}$ of 12	$\frac{1}{4}$ of 12
Fraction Pie **D**	Fraction Pie **E**	Fraction Pie **F**
$\frac{3}{4}$ of 12	$\frac{1}{3}$ of 12	$\frac{1}{6}$ of 12
Fraction Pie **G**	Fraction Pie **H**	Fraction Pie **I**
$\frac{5}{6}$ of 12	$\frac{1}{3}$ of 15	$\frac{2}{3}$ of 15
Fraction Pie **J**	Fraction Pie **K**	Fraction Pie **L**
$\frac{1}{5}$ of 15	$\frac{2}{5}$ of 15	$\frac{3}{5}$ of 15
Fraction Pie **M**	Fraction Pie **N**	Fraction Pie **O**
$\frac{4}{5}$ of 15	$\frac{1}{2}$ of 16	$\frac{1}{4}$ of 16

Extra Practice Math Centers: Multiplication, Division, & More © 2007 by Mary Peterson, Scholastic Teaching Resources

Fraction Pie P	Fraction Pie Q	Fraction Pie R
$\frac{1}{3}$ of 9	$\frac{2}{3}$ of 9	$\frac{1}{2}$ of 10
Fraction Pie S	Fraction Pie T	Fraction Pie U
$\frac{1}{5}$ of 10	$\frac{2}{5}$ of 10	$\frac{3}{5}$ of 10
Fraction Pie V	Fraction Pie W	Fraction Pie X
$\frac{4}{5}$ of 10	$\frac{1}{2}$ of 8	$\frac{1}{4}$ of 8
Fraction Pie Y	Fraction Pie Z	Fraction Pie AA
$\frac{3}{4}$ of 8	$\frac{1}{2}$ of 6	$\frac{1}{3}$ of 6
Fraction Pie BB	Fraction Pie CC	Fraction Pie DD
$\frac{2}{3}$ of 6	$\frac{1}{6}$ of 6	$\frac{5}{6}$ of 6

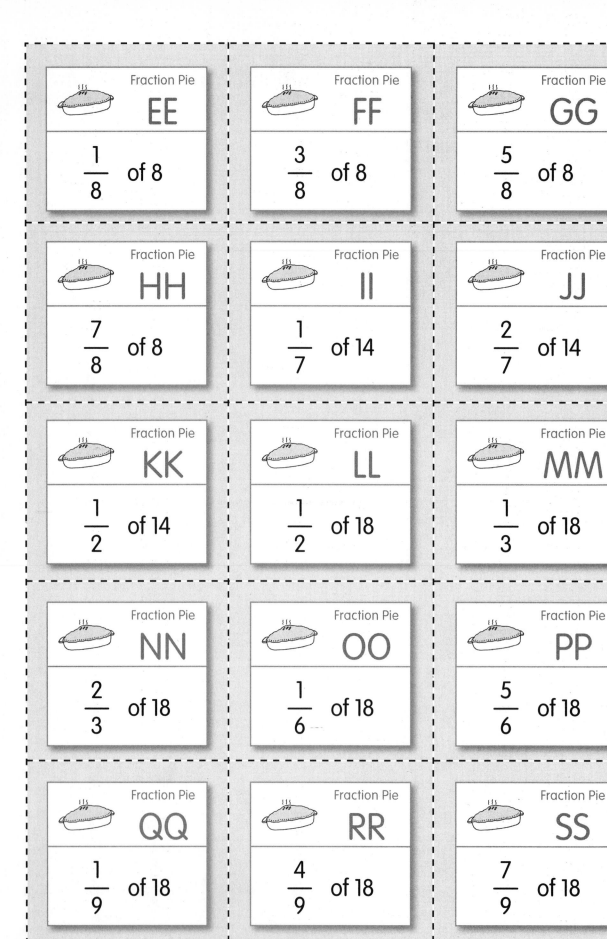

Fraction Pie EE	Fraction Pie FF	Fraction Pie GG
$\dfrac{1}{8}$ of 8	$\dfrac{3}{8}$ of 8	$\dfrac{5}{8}$ of 8

Fraction Pie HH	Fraction Pie II	Fraction Pie JJ
$\dfrac{7}{8}$ of 8	$\dfrac{1}{7}$ of 14	$\dfrac{2}{7}$ of 14

Fraction Pie KK	Fraction Pie LL	Fraction Pie MM
$\dfrac{1}{2}$ of 14	$\dfrac{1}{2}$ of 18	$\dfrac{1}{3}$ of 18

Fraction Pie NN	Fraction Pie OO	Fraction Pie PP
$\dfrac{2}{3}$ of 18	$\dfrac{1}{6}$ of 18	$\dfrac{5}{6}$ of 18

Fraction Pie QQ	Fraction Pie RR	Fraction Pie SS
$\dfrac{1}{9}$ of 18	$\dfrac{4}{9}$ of 18	$\dfrac{7}{9}$ of 18